CW00866198

JANNER ON CHAIRING

Janner on Chairing

Greville Janner
QC MP

Gower

Published by
Gower Publishing Company Limited
Gower House
Croft Road
Aldershot
Hants GU11 3HR
England

Gower Publishing Company
Old Post Road
Brookfield
Vermont 05036
USA

British Library Cataloguing-in-Publication Data

Janner, Greville
    Janner on chairing
    1. Meetings. Chairmanship. Manuals. For
    management
    1. Title
    658.4′563

    ISBN 0–566–02752–6

Printed and bound in Great Britain by
Biddles Ltd, Guildford and King's Lynn

Contents

Contents

17 Compromise   55
18 Who speaks?   58
19 Handling disruption   60
20 Coping with anger   64
21 Opponents and enemies   67
22 Plants – and their dangers   72
23 Interruptions   75
24 Time management   78

Part IV Rules and Procedures
25 Precedents   85
26 The agenda   89
27 Minutes   92
28 Adjournments   96
29 Resolutions, motions and amendments   98
30 Votes   102
31 Elections   106
32 Resignations   109
33 Trespassers   112
34 Order! Order!   115

Part V Special Occasions
35 Chairing conferences   121
36 Administering conferences   125
37 Chairing the company   128
38 Winning a beauty contest   134
39 Meals and social functions   139
40 Creditors' meetings   143
41 Ceremonial and commercial   145

    Checklist for the Chair   148
    Chapter summaries   150
    Index   169

Preface

The success or failure of a meeting depends on 'the chair'.
If you are in that hot seat, you hold as much responsibility for guiding that gathering as the captain does for
his ship. You are the master of ceremonies, in charge of
both ceremony and content; and the compère, deciding
who speaks and when and for how long. The meeting
will reflect your method, your manner and, above all,
your mood.

In the chair, you operate the procedures of your organisation. You must know them, and understand how to
use them sensibly, sensitively and flexibly.

Whether you are voted into or appointed to the chair
– even if you are self-appointed – yours is the challenge
and the responsibility. Failure is inevitable for the unin-
itiated, the inexperienced, the untaught, or the unwary.
It is also a danger even for the skilled, the schooled, and
the experienced.

Chairing meetings, then, is a science and an art, both
of which deserve to be taught and learned. Too often
they are neither.

This book is designed to provide you with the tools of
the trade. It charts the paths to success and identifies
the traps to avoid. It explains the structure and layout

of gatherings, as seen from the chair, from preparation
at the one end to post-mortems at the other.

Above all, this book explains how to win a meeting
from the chair; how to get your own way, with goodwill;
how to steer a meeting.

In the course of some 30 years in public and business
life, I have chaired a remarkable variety of meetings,
from intimate gatherings with company colleagues to
huge rallies in Trafalgar Square, from legal powwows to
political boxing bouts. For six years, I presided over the
Board of Deputies of British Jews, an ancient and distinguished body which has always prided itself on con-
sisting of several hundred presidents, each convinced
that he or she could handle the chair infinitely better
than the current elected President.

I have also, and far more often, sat or stood when
others were in the chair. I have watched, for instance,
three excellent Speakers control that most mercurial and
difficult of bodies, the House of Commons. I have
attended meetings controlled by gifted company chair-
men, by senior barristers, and by politicians. I have
observed their methods and tried to learn from them.

In this book, I present a distillation of these lessons,
some culled from my own trials and the errors which I
have imposed on audiences under my guidance, some
from the successes and failures of others in the chair. I
hope that if you are in the chair and both know and
follow the rules and the advice in this book, you will do
credit to yourself and justice to those who have either
put you in command or were prepared to accept your
leadership.

This book draws on my own experience and that of my
colleagues in JS Associates – Paul Secher, Daniel
Janner, Caroline Janner, Leslie Benson, Anthony Col-
eman, and John Balsdon – with whom I have long taught
top executives and professionals the art of Presentational
Skills. Our victims have, we trust and believe, learned
much from us. We in our turn have learned more from
them. Those lessons, too, are encapsulated in these chapters. Both the ethics and decencies of our professions and

the laws on defamation have (I hasten to reassure them) ensured that neither the individual nor the organisation is recognisable!

Curiously, my main technical difficulty in writing this book results from the sexism on the subject. In the wake of such monumental and Amazonian world political figures as Indira Gandhi, Golda Meir and Margaret Thatcher (all of whom I have watched at work and some of whose techniques appear in this book), how could it be 'Janner on Chairmanship'? In a legal scene which bans (for instance) advertisements for postmen, waiters or manageresses, how can I justify naming an occupation as if it were masculine?

One alternative to 'Janner on Chairmanship' is 'Janner in the Chair'. For someone like myself who spent a year studying criminology at Harvard Law School, visiting such splendid institutions as Sing Sing and Alcatraz, that expression evokes the aroma of frying flesh.

Nor are 'chairwomanship', 'chairpersonship' or even 'chairship' possibilities. 'Chairperson' is slowly coming into sensible vogue, but still sounds awkward. Meanwhile, my readers will, I hope, accept the inelegant 'Janner on Chairing' with good grace.

In mitigation, though, I have tried in the text to breathe life into the inanimate 'chair' for those who are in it, to use 'you' instead of 'the chairman', and to make it clear as I do now that women are no more and no less likely to succeed from the chair than are their male colleagues.

This book is intended both for reading and for reference. Just as it is part of the chair's job to keep meetings alive – to salt dull proceedings with wit, to pepper with interest, and to spice with story or anecdote – so there is no reason for a book on chairing to be boring. I hope that you will enjoy using it.

For easy reference, you have crisp chapters and brisk checklists, plus a full contents list at the start and a careful index at the back.

My love and thanks to my daughter, Laura, for revising and checking this manuscript. I wish her marginal

notes could have been included in their own right!
Thanks, too, to Leslie Benson and to Paull Hejinian for
this assistance.

Greville Janner

PART I

WINNING QUALITIES

1 Qualities of the chair

Who is ideal for the chair? What qualities should you cultivate, if you have your eye on, or your rear in, the chair? Or if you have a choice of people to put into the chair, without past performance as a guide, whom should you choose?

Start with qualities of fairness. As detailed in Chapter 4, the chair must be fair. No one is without bias, but fair people recognise their own prejudices and make allowance for them. Where appropriate, they declare their interest: 'I will now give you the benefit of my own, well-considered bias!' Or at least, in recognising that bias when making their judgements, they lean against it.

If you want to be appointed as a Justice of the Peace, your qualities will be assessed by individual JPs and by a committee of magistrates. They will be looking for intelligence, experience and common sense – all of which are also necessary qualities for the chair. But above all, they will assess you for that quality of fairness without which there can be no justice.

The person in the chair dispenses justice among the participants. Many brilliant and otherwise excellent people are incapable of fair judgement and therefore unfit to preside.

Self-control is the next obvious prerequisite for control of a meeting or gathering. The more turbulent the

3

throng, the greater the stress, the more difficult the problem, the more urgent the circumstances, the more poign-
ant the attack, the greater the need for calm.

Any loss of temper must be deliberate. There are many
occasions when you will feel anger and a few when it is
appropriate and helpful to show it. So even anger must
be carefully controlled. The moment you lose your head,
you lose your meeting and your case.

If you are blessed with a calm and happy disposition,
self-control may be easier. But there is nowhere more
open to provocation than the chair.

As a wartime schoolboy, I was evacuated to Crow-
thorne, a village near Broadmoor. I was billeted with the
family of a kindly warder, and cycled each day to the
mansion converted into a school building. During the
snowy season, we released our aggression by throwing
snowballs at pupils from the nearby Wellington School.
One day, Walter Oakeshott, that most calm, fair and
relaxed of headteachers, chided us as follows: 'I do feel
most awfully strongly', he smiled, 'that boys should not
throw snowballs at Wellingtonians. Unless, of course,
under the most extreme provocation!'

There are occasions when self-expression is permissible even from the chair, but only rarely. If you
strike someone and are charged with assault, reasonable
self-defence is a good legal defence. Provocation is not.
It may reduce your sentence, but cannot prevent
conviction.

To show your convictions in the chair, do not respond
to provocation with aggression. Like the psychiatrist or
analyst, recognise that the only way to deal with hostility is generally by cool, calm response.

Which leads us to swiftness of clear and objective reaction. A good chair is able to sift out the reality of a
problem; to burrow into the depths of an argument and
to fish out the real issues; to sort out, recognise and
advocate a sensible solution.

As a young barrister, I relied greatly on the kindness
and guidance of a wise and genial senior colleague,
Charles Lawson, who later became a most excellent Old

Bailey judge. I was amazed at the speed and concentration with which he would devour a vast pile of papers. 'What's the art?' I asked him.

'First, my boy,' he said, 'understand that the dangerous briefs are the little ones. Where you have a pile of rubbish, you can shoot through it. If the solicitors have given you all the information, you can find your way round very swiftly. And you'll soon learn that, however massive a case, there are invariably only one or two points which will decide it. The trick is to spot them!'

As with briefs and cases, so with meetings and gatherings. You must spot the key problems and solutions, the essential points at issue; concentrate your mind and the attention of the meeting on them. Once a point is spotted, a cunning chair may wish to steer the meeting away from it. That too requires an ability to stand back, assess the problem and the situation and to act – or avoid acting – accordingly.

The next winning quality is understanding procedures. A good chair will know the procedures of the organisation and how they are by tradition operated and made acceptable. The basic procedural ground rules are in Part IV. Before you chair, you should know them, so that you apply them by conditioned reflex. And always have an experienced company secretary or an informed ally at your side.

The cement for all these qualities and the margin for inevitable error lies in a highly developed and carefully used sense of humour. A shaft of kindly wit can diffuse a crisis, calm a storm, and create goodwill out of ill humour.

Finally: like all other successful operations, chairing needs good fortune. You cannot win them all, but if you are one of those fortunates who can tempt the winds of providence to blow in your direction, you deserve to succeed. And if you are choosing someone to lead your meeting, look for someone who is lucky, because this person will have the clever mind and calm temperament that always bring good fortune – in and out of the chair.

2 Where the buck stops

The chair holds the ultimate responsibility. If your meetings are in order and successful, as chair you may take much of the credit. But the troubles, too, are yours.

I once asked a safety officer to define his job. 'I am in charge of accidents!' he replied.

The chair is in charge of disasters, but to define your role in this way is to admit defeat. The ability of the chair to handle this responsibility in times of crisis — that is the true test of leadership. That is when your mettle is tested, when toughness is on trial. This is when, to adopt the American cliché, the buck stops here.

So how do you develop and harden those qualities you need in the chair? Not for you the courses and challenges imposed by armed forces on those who aspire to lead in battle. Not for you the training which you, as a leader in industry, commerce or the professions, impose on others. You are expected to pick up your complex and demanding job through trial and error. The errors will therefore be yours, and the trials those of your victims.

First suggestion, then. Why not be the exception to this traditional, British rule? My colleagues and I are among those who train people in the presentational and organisational skills required in the chair. We cover the

entire ground, even showing how to handle the confront-
ational interview on TV, radio, or by the press.

Take clients who are brilliant in business, experts in
finance or computing or company organisation or in any
other specialised field. They find themselves out front,
responsible. Recognising that it is irresponsible to
attempt the job without at least learning how to appear
confident and in control, they have the modesty to learn
that which others are trained to teach. Anyway, whatever chair you occupy, at least have the humility to know
that when you stop learning, you are old. And anyway,
the greatest fun in life comes from learning and doing
something new.

Next, watch others chairing and learn from them –
hopefully from their skills, but otherwise from their
fumbles. At best, you can succeed where they fail. At
worst, using your critical facilities will help while away
dull hours.

Then, study the techniques in the cultivation of that
apparent and later real confidence which brings style
and control in its wake. Most of this book is devoted to
the tricks of that trade.

Finally, and most important, look to the real and ultimate aims of your particular exercise. A speech or other
presentation must be designed for and targeted at its
audience. As such it must understand that audience.

What are the aims of your organisation, your meeting,
your own effort and time and devotion? You are there to
serve a cause.

If you do not enjoy the chair, you will do the job badly.
Do not feel guilty if you find fulfilment in your work
because you will not fulfil your role in the chair with the
distinction and devotion it deserves.

Whatever your immediate object, in the end what matters is your name and that of the body you serve. It may
take a lifetime to build up that most precious of assets,
but since the days of the Prophets of the Bible, preachers
have proclaimed that there is no asset greater than the
name that wins respect.

As the prows are to ships, chairs must be to the organ-

isations or the meetings which they not only control from
the front, but also front in the eyes of the world. Your
good name and that of your organisation are inseparable.
From the chair, it is your job to preserve and to cherish
both. A good name is easier to lose than to win and there
is nothing more vulnerable to attack by the critical,
the envious, the irritated predecessor or the would-be
successor, the maker of mischief, the creator of trouble,
the scourge or the irritant.

Do not complain, though. You are either a volunteer
masochist or you agreed to be drafted. To look on the
positive side, the combination of your position of strength
and of power, of influence and of prestige, and the
strength of your colleagues and allies, of those who wish
or who need you to succeed – these have put you on top,
out front, into the chair.

So harness, massage, encourage and promote the interests of those who wish you to win. Their desire and your
talent and position should guarantee success. If they do
not, then you are not in position and should not be in
the chair.

3 Listening and judging

As a Cambridge undergraduate, I was standing for the chair of the University Labour Club. A well-liked colleague, Brian Abel-Smith (now a distinguished professor) arrived at my room, unannounced.

'My dear Greville,' he said, 'I have come to tell you why I am not voting for you as chairman.'

'That's remarkably civil of you', I replied.

'Well,' he said, 'I'm a friend of yours and I think you are entitled to know.'

'So?'

'You are a very efficient secretary. But you don't listen, and you have no time for what you regard as non-essentials. If you want something done, you simply charge in and ask someone to do it. You scarcely bother to say "Good morning" or to enquire "How are you?" If you do that from the chair, you will not be leading a happy organisation.'

I thanked Brian for his words; told him that if elected I would try to listen better; and went on to lose the election, no doubt because too many others felt the same way as Brian did.

I learned, though. Both at the time and later as chairman of the Labour Club and always thereafter, I have

tried to listen. And when I have rushed in too fast, I
have seen the spectre of the youthful Brian rising before
me.

In the chair, then, listen. And remember Dante's
words: 'He listens well who takes notes.' It is not enough
for you to hear the words of others. Jot them down, for
your recollection – and also to flatter the speaker.

Members of Parliament often receive representations
from people with whom they disagree. Constituents and
their views are entitled to respect. As the chair, you
must have patience and seem open to the views of others.
If you are wise, you will show it by listening carefully;
noting down the main points; and then, to show that you
have understood and absorbed the case, repeating them
back.

'What you're really saying is . . .'.

'As I understand it, your case could be summed up as
follows . . .'

'I gather that the sense of the meeting is . . .'

Then, having listened and heard and expressed the
views of others, you can state your own. Having given a
fair hearing to the words of others – the individual, the
delegation or the meeting – you are entitled to the same
courtesy for yours.

Magistrates and judges take notes, partly as prods to
their own recollection, partly (and sometimes by require-
ment) so that it can, if necessary, be proved that they
have based their judgement on facts or statements duly
heard.

A witness may refer to contemporaneous notes – to
jottings made at the time. As with the witness, so with
the chair: the memory should be refreshed by the note.

'I'm sorry, Mr Brown, but that is not what you said a
few minutes ago. I made a careful note . . .'

A Queens's Counsel was once overheard saying to his
junior: 'Take a note of that, please. His Lordship has said
he will turn it over in what he is pleased to call his
mind.' Listen, note and then judge.

The next essential is knowledge and commonsense.
Thomas Jefferson described a well-known politician as

'disinterested as the being who made him; he is profound in his view; and accurate in his judgement, except when knowledge of the world is necessary to form a judgement!'

A judge is always balancing – witness against witness, statement against statement; the interest of the individual on one scale, that of the public on another . . .

As with the judge, so with the chair. A balanced judgement, based on listening and memory, reinforced by notes, and backed by knowledge of the world – that is the balance that succeeds.

In the book of Daniel, we are told of the writing on the wall: *'Mene, mene, tekel, upharsin.'* Mene: God hath numbered thy kingdom and finished it. Tekel: thou art weighed in the balances and found wanting.

In the chair you will be numbered. If you do not wish to be finished – if you are determined not to be found wanting – you must ensure that you hold the balances, firmly, fairly and with manifest sensitivity.

4 Fairness

It is a privilege to be in the chair, and one that can only be deserved through fairness. Your colleagues and your audience must be made to feel that their presence is valued; that their opinions are important; that even if they lose an argument, their contribution is useful. The power and the responsibility of the chair are partners. The dictator may get results in the short run, but dictatorships are unhappy places.

Let's start with the small meeting – the board, the committee, the group. You are in the chair. You therefore control the agenda, the speakers, the timing.

Now suppose that you have reached a controversial item. Should it be on the agenda (see chapter 26), so that people do not feel that they have been taken by surprise; and so that people who are particularly interested in that item will at least have had the opportunity to make the extra effort to attend the meeting? If it is tossed into the ring either under 'Matters Arising' or 'Any Other Business', then if anyone asks for the discussion to be deferred to the next meeting, you should consider that request with respect.

Suppose a controversy has arisen over which you must decide. Be fair. Either you or, better still, an appropriate colleague who has been dealing with the matter, should explain the facts, set out the alternatives, make recommendations, and explain the rationale behind them. Your decisions are more likely to be respected if people understand your reasoning. Being fair is not enough – you must show that you are acting safely and conscientiously.

Then comes the discussion. If there are differing views, make sure that all are heard, ventilated, listened to.

Keep your own mind open to suggestions, ideas, questions. There is no point in having colleagues if you do not listen to them. And you never know when good sense may emerge, sometimes from the most unlikely quarters.

If your own mind is made up and you wish to get your own way, then use your head more than your tongue. Try planting your ideas in the mouths of your supporters (see Chapter 22). And above all, give your opponents a fair and attentive hearing.

Remember that others may not be as outgoing or as extrovert as yourself. If you are good in the chair, you will draw out your colleagues, prodding them into expressed thought:

'Have you any suggestions, Mary?'

'What can you tell us about this complex question, Jack?'

'Mr Brown, you haven't had a chance to speak. We would greatly appreciate your view.'

'Come on, Jo. I know you don't agree with me on this, but please tell us why. You could be right.'

These people – even if they decline to speak – will not leave the meeting feeling resentful that you unfairly presented only one side of the question. If you must prevent some people from speaking because, say, time is running out, carefully explain why you are cutting things short – and allow each side a final short speech.

Those who have been heard will be prepared to listen. Those whose own views are respected will usually be willing to respect those of others. Conversely, those who are treated as rubber stamps will be of little use. At best,

they will stay away from future meetings; at worst *you*
should watch out for sabotage.

If colleagues disagree with you, hear them out. If they
are critical of your opinion or, especially, of your behaviour, then give extra time.

One of the most important tasks of the Speaker of
the House of Commons is to protect the rights of back-
benchers, not least when they are putting forward an
unpopular view. I have a happy memory of Speaker
George Thomas, now Lord Tonypandy. It was Prime Minister's Question Time. The Israelis had just bombed the
Iraqi reactor. I was among the tiny minority who
believed that they were absolutely right to do so. George
Thomas called me. I mildly suggested that surely the
Prime Minister must be pleased that there would be one
less volatile and unreliable nation in the world with
nuclear potential. The place erupted with angry shouts
of disagreement. I stood in silence, my words drowned.

'Order, order,' said George. 'The Honourable member
is entitled to be heard.'

So heard I was, however unpopular my view. I am glad
to serve in an assembly where the task of the chair is to
ensure that views, however controversial, are clearly
heard.

Judges frequently proclaim that their authority rests
on the people's belief that justice has been done. As with
courts of law, presided over by judges, so with meetings
with you in the chair.

President Richard Nixon is alleged to have proclaimed:
'If two wrongs do not make a right, try a third one!'
Those who wrong others in public, repeatedly or by delib-
eration, forfeit their right to be in the chair.

5 Leadership and teamwork

You lead from the chair. You guide from the front . Such leadership depends on the organisation, the occasion and the needs and wishes of the participants.

When someone complained to Churchill that, while a magnificent war leader, he lacked greater spiritual guidance, he replied: 'I have already appointed no fewer than six bishops. What more do they want from me?'

What they want will depend on who they are and why they have come together. The style of the chair should reflect that of the people and of the occasion.

How do you acquire the right style? You apply the techniques contained in this book. You listen and adapt, with sensitivity. You learn from experience. Then you hope that you will not make too many unacceptable mistakes.

If you are chairing a presentation or a negotiation between your organisation and another group, then you are in charge of the teamwork. The team will be judged by your apparent authority and skill.

You must ensure that the team works together effectively and that the members operate in conjunction. You have two main alternatives: either you may take a dominating role, leading off, presenting the case, summing

up, and bringing in your colleagues for advice, suggestions and specific expertise; or you may rely on your
colleagues for the most important contributions, still controlling the operation but with a loose rein. Either way,
you must select, train, prepare and brief your team with
care; rehearse with them and always make sure that
they are supportive of each other and of you.

Wily or plain mischievous interviewers often try to
set a team one against the other. Their success is a
catastrophe, and is the fault of the chair.

For instance: professional people are usually sensitive
about their fees. Some business operations have similar
problems. Watch out for the sort of cross-examination,
directed at different team members and, as often as the
interrogators can manage, at those who are looking concerned or distressed:

'What are you going to charge us?'

'But you must give us some precise information. How
are your fees based, then?'

'Are these fixed fees or are you prepared to negotiate?'

'Do you charge by the hour, and, if so, on what basis?'

'Is it correct that your hourly charges are among the
highest in the country/profession?'

It is for the chair to respond, firmly and without pre-
varication. Thus:

'When we have full details of the job, we will be glad
to give you a firm estimate. Our fees are based on the
qualifications and experience of the people who will be
doing the work and the time they spend on it.'

'Yes, our rates are high, but then we are at the top of
the profession. We are the best. If we were not, then
you would look somewhere else. What matters to you,
anyway, is not the way in which we assess our fees, but
the value that you get from our work. If we did not
provide excellent value, we would not have one of the
fastest-growing practices in the country. You know that
our clients include some of the top people in the industry.
They stay with us because we do the best job.'

Watch out for questions directed at your colleagues.

Do not be shy to intervene, but be careful not to under-
mine your colleagues' authority.

'You have asked John Brown. I'll answer that, if you
don't mind. It will be my responsibility to see that the
job is co-ordinated . . .'.

'No, that is Robert's territory. Please would you answer
Mr Smith's question, Bob.'

As chair, you listen with care to your colleagues' contributions. Turn to the one who is talking; verbal support
may be necessary, but non-verbal may be equally important. Nod your agreement. Smile your pleasure.

Be aware that a cynical or inattentive response from
the chair to a colleague's action can spell death for the
presentation. Teamwork includes paying attention when
you are not centre-stage.

When my wife was appointed to the Bench, she asked
for some basic hints for magistrates. I said: 'Watch people
when they are not in the witness box because that is
when they will give themselves away.'

As in court, so during presentations. Those who know
that they are under observation are to likely to rise to
the occasions and behave as they believe their audience
would wish. Those who think they are unobserved will
show their true feelings.

The world of presentation and of meetings is indeed a
stage. The chair is master of ceremonies and co-ordinator
as well as taking at least one of the main roles.

When the curtain falls, the real test will come. Have
you left your audience with the message that you and
your colleagues intended?

Walter Lippmann wrote this obituary on the death of
Franklin Roosevelt: 'The final test of a leader', he said,
'is that he leaves behind him in other men the conviction
and the will to carry on . . . The genius of a good leader
is to leave behind him a situation which commonsense,
without the grace of genius, can deal with successfully.'

In the ultimate, the test of your leadership will emerge
when you are gone. Meanwhile, you will have plenty to
occupy your mind.

6 The autocrat

Asked about how a well-known figure performed in the chair, a colleague replied: 'He's an autocrat.' This was no compliment. According to the *Shorter Oxford Dictionary*, 'autocracy' means 'self-sustained power... absolute government...' An autocrat is a 'monarch of uncontrolled authority; an absolute, irresponsible governor.'

The nineteenth-century author Alexander Herzen described communism as 'a Russian autocracy turned upside down'. He added: 'Russia's future will be a great danger for Europe and a great misfortune for Russia if there is no emancipation of the individual.'

When the chair is perceived as an autocrat, the participants will forfeit their independence of decision so they can remain part of the meeting. They silence themselves.

Canada's wartime Prime Minister, William MacKenzie King, said: 'Government, in the last analysis, is organised opinion. Where there is little or no public opinion, there is likely to be bad government, which sooner or later becomes autocratic government.'

A meeting, in the last analysis, is organised people. If their public opinions are kept to themselves, their private opinions of the chair are likely to be as unfavourable, as the bad government of the meeting has ensured.

18

There may be occasions when it is necessary to dominate from the chair. You may have to ram through motions or decisions, if you can find no better way to achieve results.

When time is the enemy, then democracy may have to be suspended, as you drive the meeting to achieve its goal before it reaches its end. Accusations of excess strength are sometimes preferable to complaints of undue weakness. But 'chairing' and 'overbearing' are not synonymous. The aim is to win by consent.

Democracies may be less efficient than dictatorships but they are far pleasanter to live in. Where the participants in a meeting have the option of staying away, they are unlikely to choose to stay in a gathering run by an autocrat. If their voices are unheard, they may choose to be unseen.

PART II

THINKING AND SPEAKING

7 When the chair speaks

Making a speech from the chair? Opening or closing the meeting? Or presenting the case for or against some proposition? Then here is a checklist. Use it to improve your chances of achieving your ends.

- Have you prepared your subject? Do you know your case? Have you decided how best to present it?
- Have you identified your allies – and primed them to assist, whether by adding their voices or their applause or by asking the questions which will help? And what of your opponents or enemies – how will you best deal with and disarm them?
- Have you prepared yourself? Are you equipped with the necessary notes, documentation and visual aids? What will you wear to suit the occasion, the audience, the image you will wish to project?
- Whom will introduce you and how? Should you provide a CV or a note, or details of points that you would like the chair or the introducer to make, so as to bolster your case or to help you to make your point?
- At what time should you arrive? Should you check the venue, the microphone or other equipment, the

23

seating arrangements? If not, then who will do it for you and whom do you bring with you to act as your assistant, organiser, aide or liaison?

- Have you consulted your colleagues and allies – and the meeting's organisers, if they are on your side – to work out how best to put across your message?

This kind of preparation cannot be neglected – the chair who confidently hopes to cope with situations as they arise will find himself too swamped with problems to command the attention of the group.

8 Structuring speeches

From chair or floor, you must structure your speeches. Say what you are going to say; then say it; then say what you have said.

As a start, transfer your structure onto cards. Make your notes and follow them, but flexibly.

Even if you are making a formal speech from the chair or an introduction in which any false word may be thrown back at you, try to avoid word-for-word preparation. Find your words on paper and you will lose your audience. Instead, use notes.

Notes should be brief, clearly legible and written or typed on cards which you can comfortably hold in one hand. Start with your opening, so that you will be reminded of your first words, even if these are only 'Ladies and gentlemen'.

If you run into protocol, take a leaf out of the toastmaster's book and (if necessary with his help) list your listeners: 'Mr President, my Lord Mayor, my lords, ladies and gentlemen . . .'

Think broadly about what you want to convey. Work out the main points of your speech or introduction; put the skeleton of your presentation onto cards; and then turn out the words, to fit both the audience and its reaction.

I once asked a well-known orator, after a brilliant and noteless oratorical performance, whether he ever prepared his speeches, word for word. 'Never,' he replied. 'I work out half a dozen ideas and then hope for the best. Usually the words cascade. Sometimes they don't – that is the challenge of public speaking.'

I have never heard him lose on his feet. Those who read their speeches seldom win.

I asked Lord Stockton, the former prime minister Harold Macmillan: 'How do you prepare your speeches? What are your techniques?'

He replied: 'I don't use notes. I never did use them much, but now I'm nearly blind. What I do is to work out the half-dozen main points and get them clear in my mind. Then I spend some time on the beginning and on the end.'

Do that. Work out the structure and then make sure that it flows – from your mind onto cards, from the cards into words.

Once you have prepared and noted the body of your speech, work out its ending. Your first and your last words are the most important. The first create the atmosphere and the last leave your listeners with your message in their minds. Most untrained speakers lower their voices at the end of most sentences and leave their audiences at the end of their speeches on some such unoriginal and crashing anti-climax as: 'Thank you very much for listening to me.' The idea of reaching your climax before your intercourse begins is a curious reversal of nature! Your audience should be thanking *you* for addressing *them*.

From the chair, it can do no harm to thank the participants for attending the meeting; but do not use this as an excuse for omitting your message. Send people away with the theme, the intent, the decisions, transferred from your tongue to their minds – and hopefully, from their minds into action.

9 Wit and humour

To puncture the pompous, to control the difficult, to calm the meeting, humour is a massive weapon. And to do so without hurting or humiliating the target of your shafts, that is the ultimate art.

Wit is the spice of any good session. Use it with skill and discretion and it will banish dullness and breathe life into the most miserable occasion. You abuse it at your own risk.

The best humour is immediate and reactive. It emerges from the moment with apparent spontaneity. The sharp response to an interruption of the unexpected reference to the name of the venue or even to the event of the day may seem weak in retrospect, but will bring a chuckle or even a cheer at the time.

The best humour is topical. The worst is offensive. Poke fun at yourself, but leave jokes about others to them. Poor taste is seldom forgiven.

In general, leave Irish jokes to the Irish; but no one objects to the friendly and the whimsical. For instance, if you are either starting late or determined to be brief, tell them about the man who asked the Irish professor: 'What is the Gaelic for *mañana*?' The professor replied:

'In the Irish language, we have no word which expresses
quite that sense of urgency!'

You have to judge your audience before telling jokes,
especially if they can be seen as in bad taste or derogatory. A sophisticated or a young audience will tire of
light humour, while others will be offended by anything
beyond the most obvious jokes. If you tell political stories
or jokes then be sure your audience understands your
intentions. When in doubt, find a more neutral topic. An
offended listener will quickly turn against you.

Mind how you speak ill of your audience, even in jest.
When I lecture on law or on presentation, I invariably
tease my audience. I apologise in advance. I tell them
how I once ironically asked a man who had given a
particularly cunning answer to a question: 'And when,
sir, were you last in prison?' 'I was released three weeks
ago!' he replied. You tread on the dignity of others at
your risk.

To use humour effectively, you must combine two conflicting elements: familiarity and recognition, on the one
hand, and surprise, on the other.

While humorous speakers must not collapse in laughter at their own jokes, they should usually smile or otherwise indicate to their audience that they are jesting. But
equally, it is the element of surprise that brings down
the house, particularly when the joke has an extra sting
in a second tail.

Timing and confidence are the twin keys to success
with humour – plus experience. Do not be afraid of the
after-dinner speech. Practise it. If giving a serious talk,
anywhere other than at a funeral, slot in some humour.
The less it is expected and the more boring the occasion,
the more it will be appreciated.

Finally: if humour fails, switch off. Do not be upset.
Audiences can be fickle and unpredictable.

So if your audience is in no mood for humour, go serious. If it begins to yawn, brighten its mood with a joke
or a jibe, a tale or a twist. Watch your audience like a
hawk or your humour will drop like a stone from the
sky.

Make fun of yourself and no one will be offended. Ridicule your faults and they will seem less important. Make jibes at your best qualities and you politely praise yourself. Your audience will recognise the self-confidence it takes to laugh at yourself.

Addressing a French audience in Strasbourg, seat of the European Parliament, I was asked by the charming wife of President Pierre Pflimlin: 'M. Janner, what is your origin?'

I replied: '*Je m'excuse . . . pardonnez-moi*. I am British. But it is not my fault!' The place exploded with delight.

I continued: 'However, I was born in Cardiff so I am Welsh. The Welsh are the cream of British society, in our own mind, if not that of anyone else. We are, if you like, the *Strasbourgeois* of the United Kingdom.'

The converse of running yourself down is, of course, playing your audience up. No one spurns flattery. Israeli parliamentarian Abba Eban, who is one of the world's most accomplished speakers, once responded to a particularly flowery introduction thus: 'I thank you very much for those wonderful compliments. No politician can afford to be other than grateful for compliments, however undeserved. We receive them too rarely!'

Self-deprecation is easy for politicians because everyone so readily deprecates us. Thus: 'I suppose you know the definition of a statesman? A dead politician.' Or: 'A politician is, of course, a person who speaks while others sleep . . .'

I took some American guests around Westminster Abbey. I showed them the inscription on the tomb of a deceased colleague: 'Here lies a great politician and an honest man,' it read. A guest exclaimed: 'I did not know that in Britain you buried two people in the same grave!'

The chair, like the writer, should guard his lips from guile and his tongue from ill-judged jokes. Unless they are at his own expense, they may be just that!

Those, then are the ground rules. Operating them is a problem.

For instance: you cannot always tell who of your audience will enjoy exchanging barbs with you and who will

take them as a personal affront. Chairing one organisation, I thought that a bright and witty man with whom
I exchanged public insults took as much pleasure in them
as myself, but later discovered that he was looking for
offence and had no trouble in finding and in taking it.

If, like me, you enjoy a laugh, then you will take
chances from the chair. If your humour goes wrong, take
heart. At least you may hope that most of your audience
will appreciate your effort to bring light into the darkness of what otherwise might have been yet another
boring occasion.

Still: you risk the modern equivalent of Queen Victoria's frosty response to a story which she found unattrac-
tive: 'We are not amused.'

Nothing ventured, nothing gained. No jokes, no witti-
cisms, no laughs. No chance of anyone being offended by
your humour. But what a boring meeting it will be!

Finally: a quote from a journalist's commentary on the
chairman of a Party Conference. He is 'a model of sense
and a quietly twinkling personality with a talent for
shutting up fools from the chair without being hurtful'.
That is a tribute much to be envied. Humour that is not
hurtful is a commodity to be treasured.

10 Body language

The body talks, even when the tongue is silent. When you walk into a meeting room after the chair is in position, you automatically look out for his or her reaction.

When you enter a meeting, greet the chair. If there is a smile in response, the occasion is warmed; if a scowl, you need no word to convey regrets at your arrival.

Perle Mesta, the famous Washington hostess, used to welcome her guests with the words: 'At last!' On departure she would say: 'Already!'

From the chair, you should nod, smile and indicate your appreciation of an arrival. A nod and a smile will also serve to regret a departure.

So the new arrival sits and looks at you in the chair. What is your appearance?

One of our most distinguished clients is a small man in tinted spectacles. He used to chair his company conferences flanked by two tall colleagues, upright and respectful. He slid forward until he appeared to rest his chin on the table. The Mafia chief was in position, with his minders at the ready.

We taught him to sit up; to tuck his rear into the angle between the seat and the back of the chair; to lean comfortably back, relaxed and with authority, actually and apparently alert and ready to react to his audience.

The chair itself should provide support for the back and, preferably, for the arms. You do not need a royal throne, but the principle makes sense. You must see and be seen; you must sit upright but comfortably.

If you chair an important meeting, you are likely to be as nervous as any speaker. But, like the orator, you must know how to harness and to handle your nerves (see Chapter 13). Look good. Put your shoulders against the back of the chair, your arms on the sides and look at your audience.

When you stand, do so with the same authority. In many ways, that is easier. Once on your feet, you command attention. Stand still. Wait for silence before you speak. If necessary, rap on the table with a gavel or clap your hands smartly together. Start the meeting in command.

If one individual keeps chatting or does not give you his or her attention, then say: 'Mr Brown, shall we begin?' or 'Mrs Green . . . if you please . . .'

Whether you stand or sit depends on the place, the audience and the occasion. Numbers are the main consideration. Can they see you if you are seated? Do you need to stand, to dominate? Given the choice, it is usually better to stand. Ask any lawyer who works in both courts and tribunals: 'Which is easier?' The answer will usually be: 'Courts, because you stand. In tribunals, you have to work seated.'

Words, then, are only one way to win from the chair. Use them together with your body – with techniques supplemented by practice and experience. Given the chair, good fortune and the right allies, you should be unbeatable.

11 The voice of authority

The chair must be both seen and heard. Authority requires voice as well as presence.

If amplification is necessary, then learn the simple techniques of using a microphone. If – as in most cases – you rely on your own voice production, you may need presence.

At Harvard Law School, I studied under a senior professor who was slightly deaf and hated mumblers. When some hapless and probably shy student asked a question which the professor could not properly hear, he would yell out in a mighty bass: 'Take your voice . . . and throw it against the back wall . . . and make it . . . bounce off!'

Imagine that someone towards the back of the room or hall is slightly hard of hearing. The larger the assembly, the more likely it is that someone will be deaf.

My father, who died at the age of 89, was an active Member of the House of Lords until about 18 months before his death. During his last years he was going deaf but he could not wear a hearing aid because he found that it only made matters worse, amplifying noises and unwanted sound. So he sat at the front, near the chair or the Speaker. And too often, he still did not hear. 'Would you be kind enough to speak up,' he would say.

But he did not like saying it. No one, least of all the
elderly, likes drawing attention to his/her infirmities.

Pay respect to your audience. Keep your voice up, that
it may be easily heard.

If you are blessed with a voice of ordinary volume,
which you use without effort, then you are fortunate.
Whether in the chair or on the platform, you will cast
your words forward so that all can hear. But a large
proportion of people who take the chair do not realise
how hard they are to hear or to understand.

This may be due to accent or intonation or inflexion,
regional or foreign. We may all speak English, but when
we do so in our own peculiar ways, others must tune
their ears to our meaning or it will be lost.

If your English is accented, do not worry. On the con-
trary: from the chair or outside it, you can get away
with errors which will not be permitted to others more
mundane. But do make allowance for the problems of
others. Speak slowly, clearly and as loud as is necessary.

How do you judge volume? Training is one method.
But a good colleague is another.

I was at Cambridge with Jack Ashley, whose hearing
was always poor. When he was chairman of the Labour
Club, we knew that we had to lift up our voices, so that
he could hear us. He kept his raised, so as to be heard,
and he spoke slowly, so that the accent of the North
would transfer to universal understanding and
authority.

Some years later, Jack submitted to an operation
designed to improve his hearing. Instead, it left him
stone deaf. This courageous man then decided to become
the best lip-reader in the world. With the help of his
patient and loving wife, Pauline, he communicated by
voice, and listened by eye, with only an occasional note
required to cope with difficult words.

In the House of Commons, Jack continued to intervene
and to make speeches. But he could no longer judge the
volume of his own voice, which he could not hear. So
he arranged with a Conservative colleague to give him
signals. If his speech was too loud, the colleague would

give one signal: if it was too soft, another; if it was about right, a third.

You do not have to be deaf to apply this same principle. If you are not sure whether you are speaking at the correct volume, get a friend to signal.

Most people who speak too softly do not realise that they are only partially heard. In teaching presentational skills my colleagues and I train people to throw their voices against the back wall and make them bounce off. They think that they are shouting when they are speaking at normal volume. We record their voices and play them back. They must relearn the sound of their own speech, at the right volume.

'Wherefore' wrote Tennyson, 'let thy voice rise like a fountain . . .' The voice from the chair must rise with crystal clarity, with flow and with ease.

12 The pause

The most difficult technique to acquire and the simplest
and most effective to handle when mastered is the pause.
In the chair, this means creating and controlling the
silence between your own words and statements, and
using the magic art of breaks or adjournments in the
meeting itself.

Only start a meeting after you command an attention-
getting silence. Start by sitting or standing to attention,
looking at your audience and, if necessary, saying: 'Shall
we begin?' If that will not or does not silence the group,
then make a sharp sound. Hit the table with your gavel,
slap it with your hand, knock it with your knuckles or
with a coin; or tap a coin against an empty glass. Do not
make a series of light taps with hand or coin. Leave
that to the woodpecker. If two people are talking, say:
'Gentlemen . . . Thank you . . .' or 'Ladies . . . If you
please . . .'. If anyone fails to belt up, try looking at that
person, walking up to him or her, or simply calling him
or her by name.

Once you have silence, then you can think before you
speak or act.

As with the beginning, so as the session continues.
From the chair, you control who shall speak, when and

for how long (Chapter 18). Equally important is to control silence, your own as well as that of others.

The pause is a mighty oratorical trick. It has many purposes and uses.

First, *emphasis*: you may stress a word, a sentence or a message by increasing – or sometimes even by reducing – the volume of your voice. But you should always pause before an essential word, the crucial climax, the key ending.

For instance: 'Ladies and gentlemen (*pause*). It is now my pleasure to introduce to you, our distinguished guest (*pause*) that supreme expert in our field (*pause*) Mr (*pause*) Roger (*pause*) Evans.' At the end of such a sentence, you can lift your voice for further emphasis.

Second, *attention*: whether for yourself or for the meeting, to start the proceedings or later (see above), order requires silence. 'Order, order,' Mr Speaker commands. Until the House subsides into silence, no speech is permitted.

Third, *refreshment*: an American soft drink sold millions through the slogan: 'The pause that refreshes.' People like to shift around in their seats, to have a word with their neighbours, to write notes or simply to stretch their minds or their bodies. Or simply to cough.

I was once in an awed audience of soldiers, packed together in a German hall to hear our Commander-in-Chief, the formidable Field Marshal Montgomery. Ramrod stiff in the centre, with his beret pulled sharply down to the right, Monty snapped at us: 'You may now cough. I give you half a minute for coughing. You will then be silent!'

We were told that Monty used silence to commune with the Almighty. Asked to account for his remarkable victory at El Alamein, he replied: 'I prayed to God and asked for His guidance. "What shall I do?" I enquired. And He said to me: "Monty, do what you believe to be right. I have every confidence in you!"'

I do not recommend Monty's method for the ordinary chair, but the idea of creating a period of silence from speech for an audience to cough is a thoroughly useful stunt. Or a longer respite may be necessary: a full-bladdered audience, for example, is seldom at its most receptive.

Fourth, *breathing time*: Central Television used to give local MPs 15 minutes to grind their own axes in a programme of their own creation. We then discovered that the twin arts of scriptwriting and interviewing only look easy when professionally done. I viewed my epic on the 'Dangers of Being Prosecuted for Shoplifting When You are Innocent' with apprehension. I asked the producer for his comments.

'You didn't give your victims time to answer your questions,' he replied. 'Don't be afraid of silence. Breathing time, that's what they need.'

Planted before a camera, I had forgotten the lesson that I had so long taught to others.

Finally, *thinking time*: above all, the pause gives you and your audience time to think. You are asked a tough question? Then pause before you answer. People are flattered when you think about their interventions.

You can disguise the pause, if you wish. Before an important TV interview, the former prime minister Harold Wilson was often seen pacing up and down an empty studio, practising putting his pipe in and out of his mouth, and doing so with deliberation.

Contrast the purposeful pause with the obviously distraught shuffling of papers or of feet, the swivelling of eyes, the loss of composure.

It was once said of a royal personage (now long dead): 'He filled his life with smoking and drinking, to save himself from the horror of thinking.' The oratorical equivalent is to fill the air with words.

So give yourself and your audience enough thinking time. And if you need cooling time, adjourn.

13 Fighting your nerves

A judge once declared that the difference between indecency and gross indecency depends upon the degree of enjoyment! The degree to which you will enjoy being in the chair depends upon whether you are exposed or grossly exposed. And that in its turn rests upon your ability to think in your seat.

If you are in the chair, you have great power and you are also highly vulnerable. To avoid danger and destruction, you must not allow your mind to lose its edge.

As a start, never lose your concentration. Those who simply attend meetings are entitled to their own thoughts, to glaze their eyes, to consult their diaries, to doodle or, indeed, divert themselves in any way which may make the occasion less boring. If you are in the chair and your attention wanders for one moment, something unexpected is bound to happen at the next.

In the chair you are the driver of the meeting. Without you, nothing moves. Equally, if you sleep, the meeting snores; and by the time you awake, all may be lost.

Prime Minister Margaret Thatcher was once interviewed by BBC Radio's *Woman's Hour*. The interviewer

asked her if she was nervous during Prime Minister's
Question Time.

'Of course I am,' she replied.

'So how do you cope with it?'

'I say to myself: Come on, dearie. Concentrate,' the
Prime Minister replied.

In this story, there are two morals for the chair. First,
unceasing concentration is vital to maintaining control.
Second, concentration is an antidote to nervousness.
Even the most experience performers, presenters and
prime ministers, suffer from nerves. So if you are chairing a meeting and have problems with yours, join the
club.

Every worthwhile performer must expect to feel nervous. Anxiety sets the adrenalin flowing, which sharpens
the mind and the intellect. It promotes quick reaction
and concentrated thought. You should recognise your
nervousness; welcome it, knowing that it will heighten
your resources; and to harness and control it, follow the
same rules that you should apply if you are making a
speech or presentation.

As a start, make eye contact. Look at your audience,
as a group and individually. Once your eyes are in theirs,
they will not know that you are nervous. Conversely, if
you avoid their eyes you will at best appear ill at ease
and, at worst, shifty and unworthy of trust.

So start the session by taking command – of yourself
and of your audience. Sit up, look up and speak up.

Before you can ensure a hearing for others, you must
win one for yourself. To project your personality, you
must throw your voice. Naturally, if you face a microphone, you must make sure that it is working and at
the right volume. Otherwise, do not be afraid to speak
loudly.

The sound of your own voice will help you to play
yourself in, to give you the confidence that you need to
do your job. Listen for yourself; observe others listening
to you; and you will then relax.

You can only achieve the confidence you need for
prompt reaction by thorough preparation (see Chapter

7). That certainly includes having your papers neatly before you, readily available and (literally) at your fingertips.

Nothing is worse for a meeting than a chair who fumbles. Disarray that starts with the fingers moves swiftly to both mind and tongue. But if the documentation is to your knowledge precisely where you may need it, your thoughts will follow. Thinking on your seat requires efficient paperwork on your table.

Next, recognise your own need for guidance and support. Ensure that your right-hand man (or woman) is at your right hand. Like you, your company secretary or another top official should be fully prepared for battle.

With support to lean on – well-prepared notes and the discipline to stand up strong and look into the eyes of your audience – you will discover that nobody else can see the butterflies in your stomach and they will soon disappear.

14 Props

In the chair, you will take notes. But before you start your meeting, there are some which must be pre-prepared. The essential notes for the chair are:

- The agenda – the order of proceedings (see Chapter 26).
- Notes for the chair – item by (especially, contentious) item, prepared by the company secretary or other expert, if necessary in conjunction with the person who will chair the meeting – that preparation being of itself a useful discipline, forcing attention to likely problems.
- Names and details of any speakers.
- Notes of opening address, introduction to item or other contribution from the chair.
- Special notes on specific items.

If the meeting is of size and substance, the secretary (of the company, organisation, etc.) should sit beside the chair, checking the agenda and feeding through notes on items and speakers as they are required, so that the chair can fully concentrate on controlling the meeting.

Lay out the agenda and other notes and documents on the table, preferably in advance and in easily

distinguishable order. Those who enjoy the destruction
of a meeting take much pleasure in the distraught shuffling of untraceable papers by the person who, in command of neither self nor meeting, should be controlling
both. Try stapling coloured attachments to vital documents, especially those that are themselves small.

A lectern, be it a table or standing model, may be
useful for any speaker faced with a lengthy performance
or the need to read. It makes for easier handling of notes
and papers, which are brought nearer to eye level. It
also helps conquer the wandering or gesticulating hand
syndrome.

Desk lecterns, folding and portable, or solid and firm,
may be obtained from specialist suppliers or built by
your local handyman or carpenter. The table variety
takes valuable space when you stand and blocks your
view when you sit, and you cannot move away to the
standing lectern.

Lecturers and guest speakers, though, may prefer to
work from a lectern. For a large hall, the self-standing
lectern should be one with built-in light and (at best)
attached microphone.

If you are in the chair, organise minimum distractions
from the job of chairing. Notes, lighting, and amplification should leave you as free as possible to concentrate
on your job.

If you speak from the chair, then use notes as your
signposts, to set out the main ideas, briefly and clearly,
so that you can see them at a quick glance. They may
also include key phrases. They *must* include, written
large and clear, any names to be referred to which you
may forget.

Notes should be on cards. Postcard size is best. They
can then be:

- easily held in one hand;
- simply shuffled, if you decide in advance to change
  the order of argument or presentation;
- conveniently added to, if you keep additional cards

handy, preferably in a pocket, or subtracted from, by throwing any unwanted item away;
- put aside as the talk or speech proceeds and the subject is either covered or, in the flow of the talk, omitted; and
- checked – in a break in the flow, perhaps (most happily) during applause or laughter – to ensure that crucial items or arguments are not omitted.

The main errors made by note users are:

- Allowing others to prepare their notes. By all means get colleagues, subordinates or researchers to prepare the material, but make your own notes. You can recognise and refer to them and they can lead to any other documents from which you may wish to quote, or to which you may have to refer in order to cope with questions or interruptions.
- Including too much detail in any one note. At best, each card should bear only half a dozen words.
- Invisible writing – which includes typing. Cards should have few words, boldly written, with attention drawn to key items by coloured underlining.
- Inflexibility – or believing that notes must be followed. The great advantage of notes over scripts is flexibility. Do not lose it. Notes are guides, pointers, aids – not crutches or stretchers. Be their master, not their slave.

Hold your notes firmly in one hand or leave them on the lectern or table. Do not look down and read them while you are speaking. Most amateurs habitually put their heads and eyes down to the notes. Professionals always either lift the notes up to the eye, minimising those regrettable moments of lost eye contact between speaker and audience, or look down during pauses in their word flow, at best during the applause that their words have earned.

Finally: think about your lectern. Do you really need one? If so, then can it fold away while you are seated or will it block your view of the audience, or the participants' view of you? If you do need a lectern, use it for your opening or closing statement. Spread out your notes, so that you can watch your audience. Then when you sit, fold it away.

It is a good rule for speakers to remove barriers between themselves and their listeners. Whenever possible, I move around the table and as near as possible to the audience. Perch on the edge of the table at the front of the platform and you may be in distance only three feet nearer your audience; but in atmosphere, you have joined their world.

The chair is behind the table. Inevitably, you have one barrier too many; do not place a lectern on top of it.

15 Introductions

From the chair, you may need to introduce yourself; and you will certainly have to present others.

Abba Eban began a speech in the Cambridge Guildhall thus: 'Those who need long introductions, usually do not deserve them. An introduction is an autonomous and independent form of literary and oratorical art, designed to reconcile the conflicting claims of courtesy and truth.' Getting away with a long and convoluted sentence, as only the master of the literary and oratorical arts can do, Eban sailed off happily into his usual, brilliant rhetoric. His next sentence was equally memorable: 'It is at Cambridge that I learned those qualities of restraint, civility and moderation which have been such a serious handicap to me in my political life!'

So: your first sentence, introducing yourself or others, creates the relationship and sets the scene and the tone. The second angles into the occasion and its purpose.

If you are known to all, then the most that you will need in self-introduction would be: 'I have been asked to take the chair today . . .' Or 'I am delighted to preside over this important gathering . . .'

If in doubt, then do not forget to present yourself. 'Good morning and welcome. My name is Jane Smith. I am

Director of this organisation and it is my pleasure to chair this meeting.'

You may need a few words for your own qualifications, maybe in jest. I sometimes use: 'I have been asked to chair this session because I am unique. The only Member of Parliament . . . the only Socialist . . . and probably the only grandfather in the room . . .'. This usually provokes a few shouts of: 'No, no . . .', from other radicals or dotards, at which stage the meeting is on the move.

Then you introduce your guest. Do not forget the name.

Under stress, names are eminently forgettable. At his wedding, and watched by millions world-wide, Prince Charles even managed to forget his own. President Reagan introduced Princess Diana as 'Princess David'. Prime Minister Thatcher once forgot the name of the country she was in and had to be corrected by her husband. And a Conservative woman never became a Dame because, at a Conservative Women's Rally during the 1970 general election, she introduced Edward Heath thus: 'Ladies, I cannot tell you what a great honour and pleasure it is for me to introduce to you . . . a man whose name is a household word . . . our next Prime Minister . . . Mr . . . er . . . er . . . er . . .'. Like Queen Victoria, Edward Heath was not amused. Indeed, few of us are when people forget our names or get them wrong.

I am often introduced, especially in my constituency, as 'Mr Granville Jenner' or even (in tribute to my late father, Barnett, my predecessor in the seat) as 'Mr Bernard Granner'. Indeed, during my father's lifetime, when he was in the House of Lords, people frequently did not know which one of us they were inviting to a meeting or introducing to a gathering or even to whom they were writing. I treasure, framed in my toilet, a letter from a constituent who was taking no chances. Addressed to 'The Rt Hon. Lord Greville Janner MP', it began: 'Dear Sir or Madam'.

When introducing myself in the chair or, especially, when others introduce me (probably with that beloved cliché: 'The distinguished son of a distinguished father'), I use those stories. Develop your own.

How, then, do you remember names? No problem.
Write each one in large letters on a card and prop it up,
in full view. Perhaps on top of a glass or a lectern, but
always clearly visible.

It is even possible, as I recently found, to forget the
name of Her Majesty the Queen. And all because a toastmaster threw me off course.

For the son of a peer, the formal (if archaic and seldom
used) introduction is by the courtesy title of 'The Honourable'. A Queen's Counsel, in the mouth of a toastmaster
at a formal occasion is: 'One of Her Majesty's Counsel,
learned in the law'. And a Member of Parliament is just
that.

At a Mansion House banquet, where I was to propose
the loyal toast – 'Lord Mayor, My Lords, Ladies and
Gentlemen: the Queen' – the toastmaster fluffed the
introduction because he was not concentrating. It
emerged as 'Pray Silence for the Honourable Greville
Janner, one of Her Majesty's Members of Parliament.'

My wife had teased me for writing down my amazingly
unforgettable few words and placing the card on the
wine glass. She was wrong. Triggered by the unusual
introduction and thrown by the sea of staring faces on
penguin bodies, my stomach gave that heave, familiar to
all presenters, however experienced. Happily, the notes
were there; the names (or, to be more precise, the titles)
were clear before me. I girded up my mind and voice and
managed the toast without disaster.

So it can happen to anyone at any time. Notes (see
Chapter 14) are insurance against the mind off-balance.
Use them, in the chair, not least for the names of your
guests or other speakers.

How, then, do you call on people to speak, when you
do not know or have forgotten their names? If you are
properly prepared, you will have a well-informed colleague at your side. 'What's the name of that man with
his hand up in the third row?' you ask.

If that fails, try: 'I call on the woman with her hand
up, in the third row. I am sorry, madam, I can't see who
you are from here . . .'

Failing eyesight and a squint may be an advantage in not identifying those whom you call – as it is when blind from the chair to the entreaties of those whom you are determined not to see (Chapter 14).

Now for the guts of introductions. Do not omit them. The height of irritating laziness is to say of a guest: 'Mr Green needs no introduction . . .' Or: 'Mary Jones is well known to us all and I shall not take your time in introducing her because we have come to hear her speak and not me. So, without further ado, I hand you over to Mary Jones.'

This always reminds me of the introduction at the Cambridge Union of a particularly undistinguished MP: 'We are delighted to welcome here Mr——, whose name is a household word – in his own household.'

Find a few flattering words for your guest speakers. Ask them what they would like you to say about their work, their experience, their interests, their purpose in agreeing to speak. Try not to read out a long extract from *Who's Who*, or from your trade or industrial equivalent.

If you ever meet senior politicians or civil servants for the first time, especially those who are well staffed, you will probably discover that they know a remarkable amount about you. Someone has sussed you out for them, dug out information to be absorbed before the meeting to help achieve whatever results are desired from you.

If you are in the chair, do the same for your guests. In part, this is courtesy, much appreciated when present and greatly disliked in its absence. This is one of the essentials of the preparation so vital to chairing (see Chapter 7).

The speech of introduction is like any other. Assuming that you have said 'hello' to your audience ('Ladies and gentlemen . . . good afternoon . . . and welcome to you all . . .'); and that you have broken the ice – with a story or greeting or humorous remark, perhaps, then you move into the normal structure:

- You say what you are going to say. 'It is my pleasure to introduce to you our distinguished guest, the Man-

ager of . . . Mr Stanley Smith . . . He will address us
on . . .'

- Then say it. You make your two or three points,
  briskly and well, whetting the appetite of the audience for the feast that is to come. You do not cut the
  ground from under the feet of your speaker by
  making the speech for him. You pay the courtesy of
  explaining the importance of the speaker of and his
  subject to the audience. 'The subject is crucial to
  you . . . to us . . . to your interests . . . to our
  success . . .'

- Then you say what you have said. You sum up. 'And
  so, to speak to us on . . . it is my great pleasure to
  introduce . . .'. Then you pause. You lift up your
  voice. And you simply give the speaker's name.
  'Mr . . . Stanley . . . Smith . . .'

Forget the clichéd rubbish about: 'And so, without
further ado . . .' Remove the horrors of: 'Put the palms
of your hands together and give a warm welcome to . . .'
Forget: 'Enough from me . . . Here is . . .'

Like the end of an overture, rise up to a climax. Like
a more restrained version of a ringmaster, a master of
ceremonies, a compère, you present, simply and with a
flourish of tone, 'our . . . most distinguished guest . . .'

Then please get the name right!

PART III

TRICKS OF THE TRADE

16 Structuring your meetings

Like bodies and buildings, meetings need structures and skeletons. Engineers, architects and builders start with foundations and structures. They start with the steel and then build on the bricks. The other way round would be impossible.

People in the chair, however, let meetings ramble unstructured through their business. Would-be orators make speeches without sound summaries at the start, central passages that flow, one to the other, or ends that resound. And presenters forget that without structure, their purpose will neither be clear from the start nor achieved at the end.

A meeting should be based on a well-prepared, carefully plotted plan, formalised into the agenda (see Chapter 26). The chair must accept responsibility for the planning, the plotting and the operation of the agenda, as for the meeting itself.

In practice, deviations may be essential. One participant arrives late, another must leave early one item must be reached, another could be left.

The first time I travelled in a giant aircraft and saw the wings flexing in a turbulent storm, I was alarmed. I pointed out the incipient disaster to a steward. 'The time to worry', he said, 'is if they *stop* bending!'

Flexibility gives strength to the structure of aircraft and meeting alike. But you must start with a structure to flex.

Next: explain that structure to the participants. Tell them how you plan the meeting to run, to be timed, to achieve its objects; then you can reasonably hope for their co-operation, based on their consent, itself founded on understanding.

'I shall introduce the subject and our guest speaker, Mr Brown. He will explain the proposal in detail. We will then discuss the pros and the cons, and we shall take questions and discussion. Then we must come to a decision. The meeting is planned to end by 6.30, but if necessary, we must continue until we reach our conclusions.'

If you chair a conference (see Chapter 35), the programme should be set out on paper. If you expect change, mark that programme 'Draft' or 'Provisional'. Once again, allow for sensible flexibility.

As with the structure itself, so with the individual portions. By all means plan and specify; but be careful not to mislead.

Not long ago, a monster computer organisation invited me to address a conference of clients in the South of France. They gave me what I believed to be a flexible subject and I treated it in my own way. The speech was apparently well received, but I discovered afterwards that some delegates had complained that it did not follow the precision of the programmed content.

Part of the fault, of course, was mine; I had not perceived, appreciated nor absorbed the required instructions. But I think that part of the problem was the inflexibility of the printed programme.

17 Compromise

The chair is in charge of compromise. Where the object of the current exercise is to reach a decision which is acceptable to the gathering, it is for the chair to steer the meeting towards consensus. Edmund Burke once said: 'All government – indeed every human benefit and enjoyment, even virtue, and every prudent act – is founded on compromise and barter.'

Acceptable compromise is the prime objective of the chair, a goal that is often difficult to reach without much patience and bargaining. You offer alternatives which move back and forth, sometimes during the course of a speech, during a debate, or even over a long series of meetings. A middle ground must exist – your job is to find it.

As usual, you start by listening. No one is prepared to climb down unheard. Contestants who believe that they have been granted a fair fight may not begrudge an adverse decision, and if they can save at least part of their case from the wreckage, they may believe that their time was well spent, their meeting will run.

For this purpose, you are the referee or the umpire. Depending on the organisation, the rules and the occasion, you may be entitled or even expected to put your own view. But if this view is to prevail, you will have to listen to those of others.

The American Declaration of Independence proclaims that governments derive their just powers from the consent of the governed. Any person in the chair who loses the consent of the meeting may forfeit the right to govern that assembly.

It may be that the decision must be specific, firm, without doubt or movement. But compromise – each side giving some ground at the side, to achieve agreement in the centre – that is the ordinary route to negotiated settlement.

Do not hesitate to back down if you have little to gain but much to lose in a confrontation. An aged peer, Lord Alvanley, was once involved in a coach collision with another nobleman. The two coachmen were at fault and each lord got out of his seat to punish his own driver.

The other peer was about to strike his careless servant, but restrained himself, recognising that the man was elderly and apologetic. 'Your age protects you,' he said.

Lord Alvaney started shouting at his driver, until he realised he faced a tough-minded athletic lad. 'Your age protects you,' he announced as he climbed back into his coach.

It is better to compromise your argument than yourself, your position, or your authority. Retreat and compromise are partners in discretion. To do so with grace is the mark of an experienced and sensible chair.

In his famous *Tom Brown's Schooldays*, Thomas Hughes wrote: 'He never wants anything but what's right and fair, only when you come to settle what's right and fair, it's everything that he wants and nothing that you want. And that's his idea of a compromise. Give me the Brown compromise when I'm on his side.'

We all know 'the Brown compromise'. It means, giving way. If the other side is the one who yields, it is for the chair to provide the unsuccessful contestant with a decent chance to save face. If dignity is preserved and humiliation avoided, he will return to argue another day. Only if you wish to get rid of him forever should you see a contestant ground down and out. In the process, you may create in him an unquenchable thirst for revenge. That is the loser's price for total victory, apparent and real.

When it comes to deciding whether or not you dissolve a business or an organisation, to buy or to sell, to hire, to fire, the answer may have to be 'yes' or 'no'. Even then, perhaps you should dissolve only part of the set up, adjourn rather than destroy, buy or sell a part, rather than the whole, give notice, rather than dismiss summarily, hire fewer, rather than none.

General Eisenhower liked to say that decent people travelled in the centre of the road because on either side there is a gutter. You should steer your meeting into the centre – on either side there lurks ill feeling. Equally, you must have to be able, where necessary, to lead your meetings into taking an unequivocal decision, allowing for no doubt. The chair is as much in charge of that firm resolve as he is of a collective compromise.

18 Who speaks?

In most gatherings, the chair decides who shall speak. How should you exercise that power?

As each topic approaches, jot down those who should obviously speak on it. Start with the proposer or proponent, then (perhaps – but certainly if there is a formal resolution or motion) a seconder. Then the prime opponent (again, with someone to second the opposition?). Then if appropriate, see if anyone wants to speak 'from the floor'. Justice must not only be done, but be manifestly seen to be done. A debate must be not only balanced, but manifestly so.

To win, your point may need pre-priming. Who has influence and is likely to be on your side? (See also Chapter 22 on 'Plants'.) 'Joe, we have to get this proposal accepted. I know you're in favour. Would you please propose it? Fine. Then who would be best to second?'

In debate or discussion or at question time, would-be speakers or questioners vie to 'catch your eye'. In the land of the blind, the one-eyed man is king. Nelson clapped his telescope to his blind eye to block out the sight of a signal he did not wish to see. In the chair of a meeting, the occupant with selective blindness hold sovereign sway.

To exclude an opponent from the floor is usually unwise, particularly if the attack is to be made on yourself. My system on such occasions is invariable. I invite the attacker to make his point. I give him as much time as he requires. If others protest at this leeway, I retort: 'Mr Brown has criticisms to make of myself. Please allow him the extra courtesy to make them as he sees fit – right or wrong, he is entitled to make his point.' Then you can turn to him and say: 'Perhaps it would be courtesy, Mr Brown, if you could make your point a little more briefly...'

Charmingly, coolly and courteously – that is the correct way to respond to the critic. To gag the opponent is to endow the argument against you with unwarranted strength. It gives its proponent the sympathy which decent people give to the oppressed. Conversely, to provide time, floor and courteous attention to those who disagree with you turns opinion towards you, deflects hostility and invites the honourable to say – to themselves and (you may reasonably hope) to the meeting – 'Well, even if a mistake was made, the criticism has been heard – so let's get on with the agenda...' You have then successfully retreated the better to leap forward.

In the chair, then, you have the power to direct arguments without even speaking out yourself. Choose your speakers wisely – allowing opponents to have their say while ensuring that your allies keep the upper hand – and you will get your way and still maintain that crucial illusion of impartiality.

19 Handling disruption

Most people who come to meetings will want the chair to succeed. There are exceptions. How do you deal with them?

When deciding how to handle a meeting, you must always assess your audience. When planning how to cope with potential troublemakers, you must treat them as individuals, on the basis of their particular objectives, style and potential.

Sometimes, people will resort to mischief for the fun of it. Most of us have a touch of mischief in our nature and taking it out on the chair is an acceptable pastime, especially if either the chair or the occasion or both are dull.

Treat Mr Mischief with his own medicine. At best, join in the fun. Exchange quip for quip, insult for insult, thrust for thrust. But keep cool and smiling.

If your good nature becomes too stretched, the audience will probably by then be on your side. They want the meeting to get on with its business. They will support you if you chide or reprove the individual or eventually tell him in plain terms to belt up.

The same person may try to achieve the same disruption by attacking your colleagues – the company secretary, perhaps, or the speaker. In general, that requires far more firmness from the chair. Experienced speakers may actually welcome heckling (see Chapter 19). You may let them get on with their own defence. Otherwise, you can say things like:

'Please direct your observations to the chair.'

'I am sorry, but I cannot allow this discourtesy to continue.'

'I am sure that you do not intend to be discourteous, but I cannot permit attacks on a member of our staff. I am responsible.'

This acceptance of responsibility by the chair is itself responsible, expected and respected. Even where the fault is not yours, you may have to accept it, especially if you are chair of the organisation and you operate on the Civil Service basis that those elected to office carry all political cans.

Do not allow the mischief-maker to take over your meeting by direct or indirect attack. Some opponents will try to take control by bending the rules – raising endless points of order or using some long-forgotten procedure. Democracy requires firmness from the chair. Your sense of humour may be your greatest asset, but it must be backed by the meeting's knowledge that you will, if necessary, assert the authority that your colleagues or audience have given you – or which you have assumed because of your position.

Watch out for operators trying to twist the meeting, via the chair. Their efforts and stratagems may be aimed at all or any of the following:

- To avoid discussion of later items by provoking prolonged argument over earlier ones.
- Conversely, to rush important but controversial items through, with little or no discussion – either so as to win on that matter itself, or intending to reach an item lower down the agenda, perhaps one which you had placed at the end, hoping it would slide by in the home straight.

- To induce you to call on people on their side or to interrupt or silence their opponents.
- To force a vote they believe they will win – or to avoid one, if they expect defeat.
- To fill the sea of discussion with red herrings so as to destroy the effectiveness of the meeting.
- To cause specific harm to you, your image, your status, your presence, your future or your cause.

Once you have sorted out the disruptive person and the motive, you can then decide how to deal with that person, how to win the meeting.

To win, you will need the consent and the backing of your colleagues or of the audience. Keep them on one side and the destroyer will lose. Once again, that requires calm, courtesy and patience. Except in the most extraordinary cases, most people will want the meeting to achieve its objects, as swiftly and painlessly as possible. They will back the chair.

If, however, you lose your temper and your self-control, you may attract the sympathy of the gathering, but your opponent will have won the battle.

With a clear mind, you can assess the best riposte to your opponents and their stratagems. For instance: if they want to rush an item, make sure that the meeting has a full chance to discuss it. 'I am sorry, Mr Green, but this is an extremely important matter and I know that there are differing viewpoints on it. Now, Miss Jones, what do you think?'

Conversely: If your opponent seeks delay, press ahead. 'We've a long agenda ahead of us. We've had a full discussion on this matter. I am going to put it to the vote now.' Or: 'Now, do let's move on. I'll ask the company secretary to look into all the points raised and to report back.'

Controversial matters can be referred to a committee, sub-committee or commission. Remember that if Moses had been a committee, the Israelites would still be in Egypt, delay of this sort is a well-accepted political stratagem.

Finally, you can call for the support of your colleagues

in controlling the disrupter. 'Mrs Brown, we really don't want the meeting delayed any more, do we?'

However you choose to enlist the support of your colleagues, try to appear rational and self-controlled. Their response depends on your approach – appear calm and objective under pressure, and they will rally to your side. Frantic appeals, on the other hand, will embarrass and unnerve them.

20 Coping with anger

If you are faced with an angry colleague, customer, delegate or other listener, how should you cope? How can you deflect that person's rage or even turn it to good account? The principles are clear enough; their use needs prodigious self-control, self-restraint and self-effacement.

There are four basic rules in coping with the rage of others:

- Listen – do not argue.
- Emphasise – and apologise.
- Offer alternatives.
- Follow up.

Nahum Goldmann, founder of the World Jewish Congress, used to say: 'Never argue with an angry man.' The angrier the protagonist, the less you should argue. Instead: listen. Give the person a hearing. Communicate your understanding through your silence. If the person is normally restrained, listen with especial care. Beware the anger of a patient person.

When the volcano has blown itself out, show and express your understanding. Think how you would feel if you had been in the same position. Even if the entire misery is based on misunderstanding, is not your fault, is open to explanation or even to challenge – wait. Your time will come. Meanwhile, try a variant on the following:

'You are right. I am so sorry. I do understand.'

'Yes, it should not have happened. I am very sorry.'

'If that had happened to me, I would feel exactly as you do. I am sorry.'

Then offer some alternatives:

'I know it's not the same, but I wonder if it would help to . . .'

'Look, I know that nothing can replace your time lost, but you we would be very glad if you would accept a complimentary copy of . . .'

'Let me try fix an alternative which will be at least as good in the long run – and which I will make sure will not cost you more.'

'Let me try and put things right for you. May I suggest . . .'

Finally follow up. If your dissatisfied customer has agreed to accept alternative goods or services, then make sure that these are dispatched on time and to the correct address. If your organisation is to perform alternative work, or your complainant is to receive a special allowance or a free replacement, then make sure that your colleagues or staff who are to make the special arrangements are aware of them.

Your customer or client already has a chip on his shoulder. Make sure that he does not become like the 'well-balanced man' – with a chip on each shoulder.

So: start by watching for the signs of dissatisfaction, for gestures or grimaces of irritation, turning to anger. Like the boxer, retreat with the punches, sway and bend. Do not allow your temper to break.

Psychiatrists, psychologists, skilled cross-examiners – all will tell you that unless you wish to provoke greater hostility, you must meet aggression with calm and with understanding. Relate, empathise, then apologise, even if you have no real cause.

Then offer your alternatives. Hope that one or more

will be acceptable and accepted. Then check up to ensure that your accepted offer is put into effect.

Now suppose that you are forced to cancel a meeting or an appearance that is important to say, a prospective supplier or, worse, customer. Follow the rules. Face the music. Telephone your apologies, personally. Explain briefly. Then stand back and listen. Understand the feelings of the jilted party. Empathise and apologise. Then offer alternatives. Another date, maybe coming to them, instead of expecting them to visit you, or perhaps suggesting another colleague or speaker prepared to take your place. If an alternative is accepted, then ensure that it is put in your diary confirmed in writing, given priority, acted upon efficiently.

Then and only then can you hope for the reward for your remedy – the soothing of anger and the curing of ill will. Listen then for those happiest of words: 'Never mind. This could happen to anyone'. Or: 'It was all very unfortunate, but it has worked out all right in the end' Or: 'All right, Janet. You are forgiven – this time!' Or, even better: 'You've done me proud. Looking back on it, I must admit that the misunderstanding was at least as much our fault as it was yours. Thank you.'

During a stay at the Harbour View Holiday Inn, Hong Kong, I was disturbed by hammering, inevitable when rooms are upgraded and improved. A public relations executive received the icy blast of my exhausted irritation. She handled the situation with understanding, and charm. She listened, silently; sympathised and apologised without reservation; offered an alternative room and checked that I was satisfied. After a good night's sleep, I congratulated her on the way that she had coped with me. 'It's my job, sir,' she said. 'We are trained in trying to help dissatisfied clients.'

Listen; sympathise; offer alternatives; and follow up.

21 Opponents and enemies

The essence of successful chairing is acceptability. People must respect you and your rulings. Unfortunately, there are exceptions even to this rule: your enemies.

A priest was called to the death bed of an Irish parishioner. 'My son, do you renounce the devil, now and forever more?' he enquired, gently.

The dying man looked up at him: 'Oh, father,' he replied sadly, 'this is no time to be making enemies – anywhere!'

The chair is no position to make enemies. If you can, avoid doing so. Unfortunately, for most people in public and commercial life, enemies are a necessary misery. So choose yours with care.

Think about your position as the chair. You could start with the advice of Nikita Khrushchev, who was asked why he had received UN Secretary-General Dag Hammarskjöld so cordially at a reception when they were in the middle of a bitter public row.

Khrushchev referred the questioner to the traditions of the mountain people of the Caucaseus: 'When an enemy is inside your home', he said, 'and shares your bread and salt, then you must treat him with the greatest of hospitality. As soon as he steps outside the door, it is all right to slit his throat!'

You may fiercely disagree with someone at your meeting – but for the moment you are in the chair. You may not be impartial, but your responsibility is to be fair and tolerant. You are the host, so treat your guests with courtesy.

How do you deal with your opponents? First, spend some time before each meeting working out who is likely to cause trouble and over what. Chat through the agenda with your vice-chair or anyone else who may be concerned. Work out stratagems for dealing with unexpected problems.

If there are regular troublemakers, handle them individually according to their past performance. Provided that you keep your head, with a little luck they will lose theirs.

Also, the chair should be patient and not interrupt others. Let your opponent talk himself out. He will be satisfied at least that you respected his views – and the audience will respect your tolerance and reluctance to get drawn into a confrontation. Only enter into a fight when you must re-establish order or prevent a major disruption

Listen to your opponents. Remember Aristophanes: 'People before this have learned from their enemies.' They could be right. In which case, you must take over their ground – or cut it out from under their feet with a word of unexpected appreciation or goodwill.

Use humour. Wit is a wonderful weapon, when used with intelligence and sophistication. It is better to hack down an opponent with laughter than with a sword.

Be careful, though, whom, how, and when you humiliate. Arthur Koestler said of the victims of such treatment: 'One can reach a point of humiliation where violence is the only outlet.' Unless you wish to provoke your opponent into violence, keep the temperature down.

Should you drive the enemy out of your meeting? Probably not. The question is always: would he cause more trouble or disruption outside than within?

President Lyndon Johnson hated FBI chief J. Edgar Hoover. After failing to get rid of him, he shrugged off the misery to a friend: 'It's probably better to have him inside the tent pissing out, then outside pissing in.' As with presidents and their tents, so with chairpersons and their meetings.

An enemy with unpopular views may be bothersome, but he will be outvoted in a meeting of your allies. From the outside, though, he can talk to the media or spread discontent through the organisation – or even persuade clients to stay away.

If your opponent has the support of the rest of the meeting, his views will probably win out. Expel him, and the rest of the group will follow – leaving you alone and powerless. Instead, sit tight and use your position to try and reach a compromise, to reduce the strength of your enemy.

You may decide to open the debate by expressing your view, so as to influence the course of the discussion from the start. You may prefer to let your opponents speak first, holding your fire until you see the whites of their eyes and the precise nature of their arguments. Or you may listen with real or apparent rapt attention to all the arguments on both sides and then pronounce your judgement, preferably as the actual consensus of the meeting: 'It would appear that the majority of us feel that . . .'

If you are met with shouts of 'No, no . . .' then you may perhaps allow the debate to continue, hoping that the atmosphere will change and calling on some of your allies – or even having another try yourself. Or if you judge that you are likely to win, you can call a vote, if that accords with the procedures of the organisation or gathering.

If you lose, then do so gracefully. Retain the poise and authority of the chair by smiling and saying: 'If that is the wish of the meeting, so be it. Now, let's move on to the next item.'

Lord (Arthur) Goodman is one of the best chairpersons in the business. I remember meeting him shortly after

the Argentine had invaded the Falkland Islands. 'The
Prime Minister has two options,' he told me. 'She can
either march down to the Falklands, with the remorse-
less tread of an elephant, crushing opposition underfoot.
Or she can flick the issue off her shoulder, like a fly.'

I have seen him use both methods from the chair. He
can crush the opposition with a charming determination
which makes any objection seem churlish and ignorant.
Or he can simply say, 'Well, ladies and gentlemen, if
that's what you want, that's decided. And we'll move on.'

How you react depends, of course, on the issue under
discussion and the importance that you attribute to it.
It is vital, though, that even those who have lost will
feel that their journey, their time, their own preparation
and effort, were at least worthwhile.

So do not allow your opponents and enemies to push
you out of the chair. Sit tight, unless you are voted out
of office, in which case you have no alternative other
than to leave, with dignity.

To sum up so far: you cannot be too careful in your
choice of enemies. Spot them early, handle them with
patient calm, and keep them in the camp. Do not force
a confrontation unless it is unavoidable – in a fight some-
body must lose, and it might be you.

Do your best, then, to see that your opponents do not
evolve into your enemies, other than by your own purpose and intent. You may disagree without being
disagreeable, and every lawyer and politician knows that
it is essential to sanity that your disputes are for court
or public forum and that you leave the battleground as
friends, dining companions, or drinking partners.

Do not equate disagreement with enmity, opposition
with dislike. Traditionally, leaders are knifed in the
back. In politics, people rarely get so unpleasant that
they knife each other from the front.

It is the job of the chair to keep opponents apart, to
substitute argument for fisticuffs, or (as Churchill once
put it) 'jaw-jaw instead of war-war'. One of the maxims
of Publius was 'treat your friend as if he might become
your enemy'. Much better from the chair is to treat your

enemy as if might become your friend – your chances of his doing so will be much greater!

In (almost) any case, a calm objective approach will subdue your adversary, at least to the point of politeness. And since you stand centre stage, he or she will have difficulty in deflecting the limelight from you if forced by your friendliness to play by the rules.

22 Plants – and their dangers

In the chair, you need allies. To win, you should plant them strategically, nurture them constantly, but be aware of the dangers they can present.

In your role as umpire or referee, you must stand back from the fray. You may be entitled to put your own viewpoint, but it will usually be better for an articulate ally to present it for you. Arrange for that presentation, in advance.

If you expect trouble from others, then plant your team at strategic points. Like the captain of a football team, place your people to mark the opposition.

Sometimes it may be better for your contingent to fan out, so that support may emerge from all sides. Sometimes you may prefer to keep the team compact. Sometimes you may have no choice. At some meetings, each opposing element tends to congregate, for encouragement or for moral protection.

Time is a big problem for the chair. How do you bring a debate to an end? How can you rein in a discussion without ill will?

If the meeting is informal, pass a note to an ally saying: 'Would you care to suggest that we move on?' If the proceedings are more formal, the organisation probably has some procedure for 'closure' or moving onto the next item on the agenda. So give the nod to an ally.

'I move the closure, Chair.'

'Thank you, Charles. But I prefer to take another contribution from each side. Is that agreed?'

Or: 'I've already promised Roger and Mary that they can speak. Let's call them and then we'll have a vote on the closure.'

I put these systems to a respected colleague with decades of experience in the chair of committees, of councils and of political groups and parties. He said: 'Dangerous. When you are chairing a meeting, it is your responsibility to regulate the timing of debates. It's unfair to try to push this onto anyone else. You must do your own dirty work.'

He could have added that people do not necessarily like to be or to appear as the poodles or puppets of the chair.

That said, the cultivating and positioning of friendly plant life is a sensible tactic for all those who wish to win meetings, whether from the floor or from the chair. You must operate with sophistication and with the help of trustworthy colleagues. But well-placed allies are worthy weapons in the constant effort to avoid battles where you can and to win them where fight you must.

Finally: a little on the art of chairing from the side. If you are the boss, you do not need to sit in the centre, or at the front, to control the meeting, its atmosphere, its proceedings or its outcome. Heads will turn in your direction if you have the power to make them roll.

Suppose that you take over a company. You wish to assume control, but (for whatever reason) to leave the current chairman in place. You attend board meetings; you sit at the side; but effectively, it is now the chairman who is the plant. He is your surrogate. Robert Browning wrote:

All service ranks the same with God:
With God, whose puppets, best and worst
Are we. There is no last or first.

Ultimately, it is not the position of the puppet that matters, but the good sense and skill of the operator.

In this case of course, you should recognise that your 'puppet' has some control. He or she, at least in theory, is in the chair. Your lead, therefore, should be sufficiently subtle to indicate that you respect your colleague's dignity, and to ensure that the rest of the meeting are not immediately aware of who is really 'boss'.

23 Interruptions

Interruptions banish boredom. Provided they do not get out of hand, they should be welcomed. Interrupters feed life into meetings; hecklers should not be excluded. It is for the chair to keep them under control.

Interruptions can be turned to immediate and to good use. An audience will back the chair, ensuring that speakers get a fair hearing. Interrupters should rally participants to your side – provided that you handle them with care and with courtesy.

If you are heckled in the chair, how do you deal with the situation?

First: ask for a courteous hearing. 'Please listen to the case. You may find that you agree with it . . .'

Bring the audience on to your side by appealing to their sense of fairness. 'Sir, you must allow others to hear the case for . . .' 'That's not fair, is it?'

It may be difficult for you to decide whether or not to intervene from the chair. If the speaker is experienced, it may be better to let him or her get on with it.

Remember Neil Kinnock's epic performance at the Labour Party Conference in 1984? He was denouncing the Militant councillors in Liverpool, who had sent redundancy notices by taxi to sack their colleagues. 'And

is that Socialism?' he roared. The place exploded and the
Militants stood and shouted. David Blunkett rose, lifting
his arms for silence, 'That's all right, David,' said Kinnock. 'I'll handle it.' Which he did. Leading Militant
sympathiser Eric Heffer walked out and Kinnock's position was assured.

With a less skilled speaker, though, the chair has the
responsibility to ensure that the meeting proceeds. The
correct reaction will depend on the size and the type of
the meeting and the nature or strength of the shindig.

Even company meetings are sometimes disrupted by
dissatisfied shareholders. The chair must handle disaf-
fection. Keep calm, cool and courteous. Any angry
response from the chair will only lead to a confrontation.
Remember to be flexible with time. Never fear to pause,
if you think the interruption can best be handled by
letting the heckler speak – and then taking the opportunity to refute his argument.

Make use of the interruption for your own purposes,
when you can. It can be a chance to confront your
opponent's views directly – and also to gain the sympathy
of the rest of your audience. A well-placed joke can show
your control of the situation and turn your listeners to
your side. Use humour.

From the chair, be prepared to deal with outside interruptions as well. An aircraft roars overhead, drowning
your words? Stop. 'Could that be (your least favourite
airline) trying to destroy this gathering, by foul means
or fair?'

Or: 'Welcome (your favourite airline). You have saved
my argument from imminent collapse! Thank you.'

If your words were not previously well received, you
will have a second chance. When the noise has gone, you
could say: 'All right. So let me tackle the argument from
a different angle. Perhaps it will appeal to you more
than the last one.'

Suppose someone wheels in a tea trolley, clattering
the cups. Pause and thank the waiter. Then wait for
silence.

A door slams or a passer-by shouts. Beam in if you can

and turn the interruption to your credit and to that of your argument. Don't lose control over your listeners. A clever joke will bring you back into the folds of attention again.

Experience will teach you when to ignore the interruption. This may be the best tactic if the interruption is minor and the moment significant; even the smallest discordant note may destroy your peroration and blunt the impact of your message. On balance, you may prefer to proceed.

If the meeting is going well, then interruption will simply break the flow. Try to reach a natural pause before you break. But if the interruption is deliberate, try to turn it to your own purpose.

With calm cunning and a modicum of good fortune, interruptions and hecklers should not cause trouble for the chair. The position itself lifts its occupant into a position of authority which he or she should not lose.

24 Time management

Joe returned from a meeting and said to his wife: 'You know I've always said that I could listen to Martin until the cows come home? Well, tonight they came home!' It is for the chair to keep the cows under control. In the chair, you are in charge of time management.

When planning your meeting, remember that most approaches and presentations take longer to make than their rehearsal suggests or that their makers allow for. Interruptions, questions and, for the fortunate, applause take up a lot of it me. The less experienced the speakers, the less likely they are to provide for the unexpected. The more self-opinionated they become, the longer they take to unload their views on the multitude.

So always allow for over-running.

Adjust the length of the meeting or parts of it to the audience you expect. By all means shorten the formalities and stretch the time for discussion or for questions. Too many meetings spend to long in discussing what they are going to discuss and how long they should spend doing it. To meet to discuss meetings is an irritation which should be left to the United Nations, where most of the delegates are at least well paid for their inaction

– and if words can avoid wars, they are worth their weight in gold.

When allocating time to speakers, always give them less than you expect them to take. If you want someone to address an audience for an hour, then say: 'Why not talk for 20 minutes to half an hour and then allow time for questions?' If you are after a half-hour exposition, give the speaker 20–25 minutes. For 20 minutes, substitute 15; for ten, seven. And if it is to be a swift interjection, say: 'Just make your point, please.'

When talking from the chair, watch your audience. If it becomes restless, either wind up or change tack or momentum. Introduce humour, tell a story, or use that most masterful trick of the confident speaker – involve your audience. 'Have any of you come across this problem? What do you think about it? Mr Green, how do you think we should handle this operation?'

No matter how many people there are in the audience, you, like the skilled cabaret artist, should extract a response from an individual. The rest will be riveted.

Conversely, if you allow yourself to overrun, then do not be surprised if in due course you will be run out of office.

When Otto Preminger unveiled his epic film, *Exodus*, he invited the comedian, Mort Sahl, to be his guest at the premier. The film told the story of the creation of Israel.

After some 3½ hours, but with another half hour to go, Sahl rose in his seat and turned to his host: 'Otto, let my people go!'

If you want people to stay, then either do not keep them too long or at least give them a break. Adjourn the meeting for people to stretch, wheel in the coffee, and if you ban smoking at the meeting then allow for the addicts to satisfy their evil habit.

If, on the other hand, you allow smoking in the meeting, give thought to those who dislike the smell. Uncomfortable people quickly become impatient and irritable. Thomas Beecham was once on a train with a famous orchestra, its patrons and directors. The woman beside him said: 'Sir Thomas, do you mind if I smoke?'

'No,' he replied, 'provided you do not mind if I am sick.'

'Now then, Sir Thomas,' she replied, 'there's no need to be rude. I think you have forgotten that I am one of the directors' wives.'

'Madam,' Sir Thomas snorted, 'I would feel exactly the same if you were the director's only wife!'

So plot and plan the time and remember that few people have ever complained that a speech or a meeting ended too soon.

How do you put an end to a speech that is going on too long? Wait for a pause, assuming that the speaker ever allows one. Smile sweetly and say, 'I am so sorry, but we have to move on. Would you be kind enough to finish, please?' Or: 'I am so sorry, but time has run out'.

At a formal meeting, try simply standing up. Clear your throat, rustle some papers in front of the microphone, and the speaker will generally say: 'Just finishing up, Mr Armstrong.'

Quietly invite a colleague to interrupt. Slip a message: 'This is taking too long. Can you help me finish up?' Your friend will stand up and say: 'On a point of order, Mr Chairman. We must end by six. Surely we should come to a vote now?' Or maybe he'll tug on the speaker's arms, and whisper: 'Come on, Mary. I've got to meet a client in five minutes!'

You could also slip a note to the speaker. 'Two minutes please.' Or: 'Sorry, please end.' But be as inconspicuous as possible. The fault may well have been yours for not giving the speaker enough time guidance before he or she began.

When you agree on a time in advance, ask: 'When you come to within, say, five minutes from time, shall I give you a warning?' Most speakers will agree – and appreciate your efforts to stop them on time.

To end a meeting from the chair is generally easier. 'Well, we've dealt with the most important items. Shall we adjourn the rest until next time? Is there anything that anyone considers that we must deal with today?'

You are not throttling discussion if the meeting applies the garotte.

Prepare for your own time problems in the chair by using one or all of the following methods:

- If you have control over the room, arrange for a clock to be clearly visible in your line of sight. Otherwise prop up your watch. If you have an alarm watch, set it to give you warning before your speech should end.
- Ask a colleague to give you an indication as your time limit approaches.
- Be grateful if someone draws your attention to over-running and never say: 'I have come all the way from Manchester to speak to you and you are begrudging me the time I need?'
- Do not speed up your delivery to pack more words into the same time. You will fail. Instead, summarise your remaining points. Pretend you have structured your address so as to fit into the time provided, leave extra time for the applause you will have earned through your consideration for the time problems of your audience.
- In the long run, train yourself to recognize and to sense the passing of time. Treasure that of others as you would have them do your own.

Remember Ecclesiastes. 'To everything there is a season, and a time to every purpose under the heaven; a time to be born, and a time to die; a time to plant, and a time to pluck up that which is planted.'

There is a time to begin a speech or a meeting and a time to end it. The closer the two come together, the likelier it is that the 'vote of thanks to the chair' will be genuine.

PART IV

RULES AND PROCEDURES

25 Precedents

Never underestimate the power of precedent. To comply with that which went before is to follow in the path of tradition, the generally acceptable route. The more hallowed the route, the less appropriate the deviation from the past.

A new American university decided to adopt the ancient British habit of reserving the grass for Fellows. Signs were erected, reading: 'There will be a tradition, commencing immediately, that students do not walk on the grass.'

More subtly, you can institute traditions by establishing precedents and then suggesting that they be followed.

In *Fiddler on the Roof*, Tevye the milkman is asked how the Jewish people have survived so many centuries of harassment and persecution. Looking up to heaven, he proclaims: 'Tradition . . . tradition!'

Iconoclasts have their place in society and radicals at meetings, but, other than in the rare times of revolution, they are in a minority. The warmth of the precedent, turned by practice, habit and custom into tradition, provides a security from which people are generally only prepared to turn in emergency.

Suppose, then, that you are faced with colleagues who are vying for a particular job, promotion, appearance or prestige. How do you decided between them and avoid a row? Look to the past. How were similar situations previously dealt with? Who was assigned to the post, the occasion, the opportunity, when the same or a similar situation arose before?

Probably, there will be precedents for any choice you make. Your job will be to pick the precedent that best fits the situation – or brings about the results you desire. If you yourself find that previous occasions produced resolutions which in present circumstances are unacceptable, look for distinctions. 'This is how we did it in such-and-such circumstances, but the present ones are very different, because . . . Therefore, the answer must itself be different. Which means that Bob must do it, don't you think?'

The British and American legal systems are based on precedent. Courts are bound to follow principles laid down in decisions at their own or higher levels. But judges frequently distinguish cases before them from those in which unacceptable precedents have been created.

On his retirement, Lord Denning was asked whether he did not twist the law to suit his own perception of justice in the particular case. 'Certainly not,' he replied. 'From time to time, I have turned the law in the right direction!'

From the chair, you must turn precedent gently, or you will be accused of twisting. The borderline between the two depends upon tactics, timing and acceptability. Tactics: who explains the apparent deviation from precedent? Timing: when – at what stage in the meeting – is this done? Acceptability: can you get the weight and concensus of the meeting behind an interpretation which should itself become moulded into precedent?

The worst situation is when precedent is against you. The next best is when you have the choice of two past reactions, one of which you wish to follow. You can then either refer to both and explain why one is now appro-

priate in the present circumstances, while the other is
not. Or you can simply refer to the acceptable one and
push the other into silence, hoping no one will remember
it.

Unfortunately, meetings are usually attended by
someone with a mischievous memory. Past office-holders
are an especial source of trouble, always ready to show
how much better matters were handled in their day than
in yours. 'In the case of this-and-that, we did such-and-
such. Which was, I think, quite right in that time and
very well handled. But when we had the same situation
in the case of here-nor-there we took the opposite view.
And I am sure that this would be right in the present
circumstances, because . . .'

Sort out this kind of problem before the participants
gather. Prime a respected ally to make the proposal,
refer to the precedent, draw any necessary distinctions.

If you are lucky, though, you will find that current
wishes accord with past actions. If so, refer to precedent
and you should romp home.

Finally: observe the same problem from the opposite
viewpoint. If you wish to introduce an innovation, then
beware of arguments based on precedent.

G. K. Chesterton said: 'Tradition may be defined as an
extension of the franchise. Tradition means giving votes
to the most obscure of all classes, our ancestors. It is the
democracy of the dead.'

To introduce innovation in the face of tradition, you
may have to be prepared to compare love of that particular tradition with the death of ideas, advances, progress.
Someone once described love of a particularly moribund
political party as 'morbid necrophilia'. Apply the same
now to the precedent you want to abandon.

An unknown naval petty officer wrote to *The Times*:
'The RAF do not have traditions. They only have habits.'
Cajole your colleagues out of habit and into innovation.

If you grow discouraged, think of the marvellous
saying of that Indian sage, Krishnamurti: 'There is
nothing sacred about tradition. The brain carries the
memory of yesterday, which is tradition, and is fright-

ened to let go, because it cannot say something new. Tradition becomes our security and when the mind is secure, it is in decay.'

If you fear that precedent, solidified into tradition, may cause the decay of your proposals, prospects, intentions, hopes or organisation, then marshal your arguments against the powers of the past. You may need them all.

26 The agenda

The organiser of the meeting – probably the secretary of the company or of the organisation – must prepare the draft agenda. It should be brought to the chair for checking, amending or approving. It is the route map of the meeting, charting its beginning, its course and its end.

When drawing up an agenda, as with preparing a speech, it is important to ask yourself some basic questions:

- What are you trying to achieve?
- How can you best achieve it?
- What should be included, and what left out?
- What problems should you anticipate and how can these be dealt with, through the agenda itself?

You will start with 'Apologies for Absence'. Curiously, an absence is sometimes more noticeable if the absentee apologises. But simply not to appear may be regarded as a discourtesy. In any case, the first task of the meeting is to register absentees.

This is followed by discussion of the minutes of the previous meeting. These should have been sent to the appropriate people before your meeting, so that any complaints can be made in advance. Anyway, this meeting must refer back to the last one and you will have to say: 'May I sign these as a correct record?' (See Chapter 27.)

The third item on the agenda should concern matters arising from the minutes. This means those matters not otherwise covered on the agenda. Tactical considerations as to whether you deal with such items under 'Matters Arising' or under 'Any Other Business' are in Chapter 26.

Next comes the main business, for which the meeting has been called. The selection of items for discussion or debate and their placing on the agenda is a crucial operation. Questions you and your allies should consider include:

- Do you put the contentious items at the beginning or at the end? Can you reasonably hope to get them out of the way before your opponents arrive – or after they leave? They can scarcely blame you if they do not turn up on time or if they have to quit before the final whistle – or can they and will they?
- Do you throw up the arguments into the winds of dispute, so that all participants may have a hearty blow, in the hope that when everyone's lungs are wearied, the storm will subside? Or can you hope to sow the wind with such speed and subtlety that you never reap the whirlwind?
- Do you 'get rid of the easy matters first', leaving the battle for the end – by which time (you hope) the meeting will be anxious to conclude, as desk, food or golf course beckons? 'I can stay here all night,' lies the chairperson. 'If you want to go on arguing, that's entirely a matter for you.' Will the meeting conclude – and if so, by doing what you want? Or are you simply asking for a postponement of an hour which will be even more evil when it arrives than it would be if (to remix the metaphors) you grasp the nettle now?
- Should you put the contentious issues on the agenda at all – or hope that they may go unnoticed? Recognising the (above referred-to) potential horrors of

'Any other Business', can you reasonably hope that the misery will pass unmentioned?

Always consider the time available. How long will items take? If the agenda appears too full, then are there subjects which could conveniently stand over until next time? Will your agenda include flexibility, in subject and in timing alike?

Alexander Pope described life as 'a mighty maze – but not without a plan'. Meetings are mazes; the agenda is the plan; if the plan is prepared with sufficient skill, care and cunning, then from the chair, you will succeed in steering participants, projects and programmes alike, out of the maze and into action. Underestimate the importance of the agenda as the chart, map or plan of your meetings, and you are issuing an invitation to unnecessary problems, which will surely arise.

27 Minutes

'Minutes!' I once heard a bored colleague moan. 'Minutes! They should be called "Hours"! They are nothing but an abbreviated record of miseries recalled!'

He was right. Minutes are a record of what happened. They record in miniature the events at meetings. It is part of the job of those who preside over meetings to ensure that the minutes of the proceedings are indeed a correct and succinct record.

As with the agenda for the next meeting, so with the minutes of the last. The responsible person – the company secretary, for example – must bring them to the chair for checking.

The preparer of the minutes wields unrecognised power. The turn of a phrase or the twist of a sentence may alter, disguise or re-emphasise the meaning of the discussion, the effect of a decision. You should check the minutes prepared by others of any meeting which you chair. The meeting and the minutes are yours.

So what should go into the minutes? Different meetings and organisations have differing traditions. Some summarise views and statements of the participants; a few (like Parliament's *Hansard*) are word-for-word transcriptions; the best are long enough to cover the essential points, but short enough to be interesting.

Minutes should record the decisions made, conclusions arrived at, agreements achieved, disagreements left over, action required. Where (as in the case of many decisions at company board meetings) the consent, approval or direction of the directors is required by law, then the minutes provide the record.

Minutes should be made as soon as possible after the meeting. If there is likely to be any argument over the precise detail of a decision, then make sure that you have careful notes. Get the people concerned to sign or to initial them before they leave the room. If necessary, read out what you understand to be the decision or resolution and then ensure that you have clear and provable evidence of the matters resolved.

In the twin worlds of industrial and international relations, too many disputes have arisen because people believed they had an argument, went home and told their own colleague or allies their own understanding of that argument, and then returned the next day to sign a record which they found did not accord with their recollection. The bargaining begins again, with mistrust compounding irritation. And all for the sake of a little extra time for recording the precise agreement and getting all parties to sign it before leaving. It is the chair who should ensure that time is supplemented by patience, where the alternative is possible dispute.

At the Yalta Conference, President Roosevelt said to Prime Minister Churchill: 'I do hope that the conference is not going to last more than five or six days.'

Churchill replied: 'I do not see any way of realising your hopes about world organisation in five or six days. Even the Almighty took seven!'

If minutes take hours but save years or avoid catastrophes, then take your time and make your minutes.

If the minutes are incorrect, then the chair must take the blame. If they have been taken by the organisation's civil servants or other employees, it is the bosses who must accept the responsibility. Which explains why the

compiler must give the chair the right and the time to
check and amend; and why the chair must not skimp
that checking. If you are in the chair and do not check
your minutes, then if you cannot explain them or their
errors, be prepared to explain yourself and your own.

Minutes should be circulated to anyone who needs to
know their contents. This normally means anyone who
took part in the meeting and in the decision making
process. Add people who should be expected to act upon
them or who will be criticised for any failure to do so.
Be careful to circularise only those who are entitled to
the information contained in the minutes. If in doubt,
send only to those who need to see the record of an
occasion in which they took part; and of course, do not
circulate the minutes until they are in their final,
checked form.

Now suppose that someone who was at the meeting
wishes to check the minutes before they go into their
final form. Normally, that is proper. Ensure that suggested corrections are submitted in advance: read and
reread them, especially if they would change the effect
of the decisions; and beware of this common and often
successful method of back-door revisionism.

If someone does ask for a correction, then you have
three alternatives. You may accept that the original
minute was wrong and alter it; you may insist that it
was correct, and refuse to amend; or you may negotiate
an acceptable form of words.

If you cannot reach agreement, then you could say to
the complainant: 'I'll leave them as they are, but you
can object when they are placed before the meeting.'
Doubts can then be placed before the memories of others.
Never forget that minutes are only intended to record
what was said or decided, whether or not any individual
agreed or disagreed with statements, or with action to
be taken.

Minute writers have too much power because too few
bother to read their work and still fewer to correct errors.
Even those who spot what they believe to be mistakes

are chary of corrections, in case they have been tricked by their own memories.

Anyway, beware of those who offer to take minutes and who may not be on your side. That is a common and cunning way to win quiet control over the decision-making process.

Finally: what form should minutes take? They should normally set out what happened, in the order of events. But the chair will generally decide on the most convenient form of that record. In general, the shorter and the clearer, the better.

28 Adjournments

One of the greatest powers of the chair is the right to adjourn. It is crucial both in threat and in practice.

The idea of returning for another session on the same subject scarcely appeals to the busy, especially those who have come from afar. So if you wish to concentrate minds or tongues that wander, try saying: 'Well, if we can't reach a decision today, let's have another go next week. Perhaps we should reconvene on Thursday? Or maybe we could get together over the weekend?'

Disappearing visions of the golf course – the apparition of an angry husband or wife, the hope of future inertia, the sheer weight of work undone – all combine to urge participants into reason.

Equally, if you are in danger of losing your way or your case, you can always say: 'Let's leave this item over till next time. We have a heavy agenda, so let's deal with . . . ? Or: 'I'm going to adjourn this discussion. It's gone on long enough and it's apparent that we are not going to reach a conclusion. So we'll try at our next meeting.'

George Thomas, now Lord Tonypandy, former Speaker of the House of Commons, was a master in the use of the adjournment to cool heads and to quell disorder. 'I shall

adjourn the House for fifteen minutes,' he would say.
The House would then drift into the corridors, the tea
rooms and the bars to recover from its ill temper. This
measure never failed.

An adjournment is simply a pause writ large. As the
orator learns the power of the pause between words and
sentences (see Chapter 12), so the chair should never
underestimate the power to adjourn.

29 Resolutions, motions and amendments

A meeting must resolve before it acts. Most resolutions are informal, most decisions taken without a vote. But in some organisations most of the time and in everybody's some of the time, formal resolutions, motions and votes are essential. The chair is in charge and must know the procedures.

When someone moves that the meeting adopt a concept or a decision, the 'mover' may propose a 'motion'. The meeting is invited to concentrate its mind and, if appropriate, to vote on an issue, set out in someone's words.

For the motion or resolution to be in order, it may have to be on the agenda, with due notice given so that those who disagree may know, attend and oppose. It may or may not be proper to put an 'emergency resolution', where it would have been impractical to give notice. All depends on the rules, procedures or 'standing orders' of the company or other organisation concerned.

Assuming that it is in order to put the proposal before the meeting, the chair will permit the mover to do so – and (again by rule or perhaps by custom) a time limit will be set. Next, someone will second the motion. If there are not two people prepared – formally or informally – to support the motion, it will fail.

'The motion is in the name of Mr Brown. He has five minutes to propose it.' Then: 'Thank you, Mr Brown. Do we have a seconder? Miss Green? Do you wish to speak or do you second formally?' If speak she will, then: 'Very well. You have three minutes.'

Then comes the right to oppose. 'Who wishes to speak against the resolution? Mrs White, you wish to oppose? Very well. You have five minutes.' Then: 'Does anyone else wish to speak against the motion?' The opposition should have the same air space as the movers.

Then: 'Does anyone else wish to speak? Mr Gold? Are you in favour or against? In favour? Fine. Please go ahead.'

Then someone on the other side. To be fair in the chair, you balance the debate. This may be easy if you know the people and their views, but the larger the audience, and the more uncertain the view, the harder your task. By all means ask: 'On which side do you wish to speak, madam?' Or: 'I shall now call someone in favour of the proposition – are you for the resolution, sir?'

'I am not decided.'

'Then please give us the benefit of your indecision!' The more bitter the debate, the greater should be your cool, calm and good humour.

Insist that the meeting respect the chair. This process begins by addressing remarks to you. Parliamentary tradition keeps opponents at tongue's length from each other on opposite sides of the chamber, with floor and table between them.

'Please address the chair,' you say. 'Through you, chair,' responds the speaker, 'I would ask Mr Green to give better reasons for his view than he has.' That statement is in order.

'That's rubbish, Mr Green,' is not.

If the speeches subside of their own accord, then you call the proposer to respond to the debate. If time moves faster than tongues, you could say: 'The arguments have been well ventilated. I propose calling one more speaker on each side.' If the suggestion is not greeted with protests, follow it.

Or someone may 'move the closure'. Then enquire: 'Shall we close the debate now?' Or, if appropriate, put it to the vote. 'Those in favour of the closure, please show . . . Those against?' If people have had enough, the closure will be passed and you call the proposer. If a majority wish the debate to continue, so be it – in the chair you are in the hands of the meeting.

If time is the enemy, remind the audience: 'We only have another half an hour. So shall we discuss this matter for the rest of our time or would you not prefer to come to a decision? It's a matter for you . . .'.

You must always try to give people the feeling that all points of view have had a fair hearing. You may be forced to strangle a debate. The balance between freedom of speech and the calls of nature, home and other business is not always easy to strike. But you must try.

However you handle debate and time, you are sure to be criticised. The best way to avoid most criticism but to deserve it most is to do least!

Anyway, eventually, the debate must end. The resolution or motion is put to the meeting. The vote is taken.

The roads to ruin, deceit and disaster are all paved with good resolutions – and with many bad ones. There are ways to avoid, or at least to mitigate, the misery.

Ban resolutions and amendments where you can. If this proves impossible, impractical or unacceptable, whether for democratic reasons or any other, then try to restrict their number or at least the time spent on their discussion.

Resolutions do have one great advantage, which should be exploited. They force participants to focus their ideas and to concentrate their minds on specific wording, to make a decision and to reach a conclusion, rather than (as one long-suffering chair puts it) 'drivelling on'. If you want to go on with this discussion,' he says, 'then how about putting down a resolution? If you don't want to do that, then I propose moving on.'

By the rules, conventions or wishes of the meeting, resolutions may have to be written, notice may be required, and people may need time to think, in which case, the respite may enable the argument to be sorted out behind the scenes or, in parliamentary language, 'through the usual channels'.

If the resolution is in order, then it goes through the usual and proper procedures, but even these may be circumvented. 'Well, Mrs Green, you have already put the arguments in favour of the motion and Miss Patel has supported it. We've had several speeches against. Perhaps we can take a vote at once?'

If resolutions cannot be avoided, they should be delayed, despatched or otherwise dealt with, with due debate and minimal ill will.

Amendments present the trickiest challenge for the chair. The resolution or motion may be altered so as to make it more – or less – acceptable, or to soften or destroy its impact.

A resolution or motion cannot be amended until there is something to amend. So any attempt to move an amendment is out of order until the substantive motion has been moved and usually until it has also been opposed. If it is obvious that the motion is not clear and that it is in the interests and with the consent of the meeting that it be amended forthwith, then amend it by consent. Otherwise, the amendement must be proposed.

If it is proposed, the procedure begins again – a debate within a debate. First, the proposer of the amendment, then, formally or by speech, a seconder; then, unless the motion is apparently acceptable to all or at least to most, two people to speak against.

When voting time arrives, the amendment is put first. If it is passed, the meeting votes on the resolution as amended; if it fails, the original motion is put.

Problems usually arise when the meeting produces a multiplicity of amendments. The same procedures should be followed with each, and if necessary, votes taken in some sensible order.

Procedural wrangles over amendments are too common and too complex. Wise organisers do their best to sort out their miseries, privately and either before or after the meeting.

30 Votes

Voting is the ultimate way to resolve differences. It gives those present three choices. They may vote in favour, or against, or they may abstain. Other than in special cases where specific majorities are required – usually by the constitution (for example, two-thirds or three-quarters for a change in the constitution itself) – a simple majority will decide.

The chair usually has the same right to vote as everyone else, but frequently declines to use it, preferring to remain at least impartial. That is a matter for the chair. In the case of a tie, the chair usually has a casting vote. Again, this does not have to be used.

In practice, persistent critics of the decision may seek its overthrow at a future meeting, their troops duly whipped into the fray. Whether another vote is permissible or permitted depends upon the rules of the organisation and the strength, firmness and views of the chair.

There are two main methods of voting: the raising and counting of hands (voting by show of hands); and the recording of votes on paper ('secret ballot'). In most organisations and on most issues, a show of hands is sufficient to indicate the feeling of the meeting.

Secret ballots have both advantages and disadvantages. In Parliament, all votes are open. Electors, parties and colleagues alike are entitled to know whether and how MPs vote on each issue. Secret ballots avoid improper pressures but mean that your opponents can knock you down without your knowing whom to blame. The smaller the meeting and the less important the issue, the less worthwhile it becomes to endure the delay and bother of written balloting. Conversely: the more crucial the decision and the larger the meeting, the more likely the need for the ballot box.

Whether or not the chair calls for a ballot depends upon the rules of the organisation. Often, you can start with a show of hands and then, if the result is close, someone may (properly or not) call for a ballot. This in its turn may be on the basis of one person, one vote. In some organisations, though, delegates on a card vote will vote for their section or organisation or union which may carry votes according to its membership (real or 'paid up' or affiliated).

If a ballot is a possibility, prepare for it. Assuming that it is to be held at the meeting, ensure that ballot papers will be available, either suitably marked off or available for marking. If there are to be several votes, it helps to distinguish between them by providing papers of different colours.

Remember to appoint 'tellers'. Impartial and respected people should do the counting, and preferably not vote on the issue themselves. Provide them with sheets of paper, pre-prepared where necessary, for recording the vote.

If hands are to be counted, this may be done from the chair. In larger meetings, though, officials of the organisation or impartial tellers should be appointed.

Special votes decide specific matters according to the rules of company or organisation. Changes in the constitution or in the rules themselves, for instance, must generally be passed by a two-thirds' or three-quarters' majority – whether it be of those present and voting or of the membership.

Again, voting is usually by a show of hands, but written rules or usual custom may require a secret ballot, either at the meeting or by post. Check the rules.

Anyway, once the mover of the motion has replied, there is no further discussion. The vote is normally taken, the question is 'put', and the matter is decided.

The chair announces the result. On a show of hands, it is often enough to say: 'I declare the motion passed – by a substantial majority.' Or: 'It is clear that the resolution has failed to secure the necessary two-thirds' majority.' Or: 'The result is very close and I would ask you to keep your hands raised so that we can have a recount.' Or: 'The result is so close that I think we had better take a ballot. I shall ask the secretary to pass around ballot papers.'

What if there is a tie? In most organisations the chair has a vote, which he or she may not use. If you are not forbidden to do so by your standing orders, you may fend off your responsibility – or nudge the meeting in the direction of your choice:

- by saying: 'We have an equal division of opinion. As this matter involves . . . I would prefer not to have to use my casting vote. So let me put the motion again – just to see if anyone has suffered a change of mind or, in these circumstances, would prefer to abstain?'

- by putting your own point of view: 'I had not wanted to come down on one side or the other, but in view of the equal division of opinion, perhaps I could tell you how I feel, and see whether that might affect the vote.'

- by adjourning the subject to a committee or the motion to the next meeting – at which (you would doubtless hope) you could rally your own forces rather better than you succeeded in doing at this one.

Many organisations avoid the embarrassment of announcing details of elections. The chair says who has been elected but does not give the votes. Others provide numbers. As usual, precedent is the best guide to the chair. 'We have always announced only the names of the winners and never the votes and I propose to adhere to this tradition.' Or: 'It has never been our custom to give the details of results, and I do not propose to do so now.'

Recounts are harrowing.

In the 1983 general election, my colleague and friend Jim Marshall was beaten by 7 votes out of about 65,000 and after five recounts.

Earlier, I had watched the votes piled on my table and that of my opponent mounting up with apparent equality. At one stage I was sure that I was out. 'I've had it', I muttered to my friend Lawrie Simpkin, the executive editor of the local paper. 'You're just in,' he predicted. 'But only just.' He was right. I was in by 1700 and Jim was out by 7.

Votes are democratic and fascinating for the observer. They are a trial and a misery for the participants. So be kind to them if they lose.

31 Elections

Some are born, endowed with or bought into the chair. Some have the chair thrust upon them, more or less willingly. Others have the more difficult task of achieving the presiding role, through the consent of their fellows. This usually means elections.

Examinations are to youngsters as elections are to others who, like me, must accept the affliction to achieve the result. Whether in business or academia, in the church or in industry, in local or national government, politics – at least in a decent society – means getting votes.

There is no shame in this. Those who seek the chair or any other office should not be ashamed to ask their electorate to vote for them. Those who are too proud to canvass deserve to lose and usually will.

As a start, you must strike a balance between apparent ambition and unacceptable indifference. On the one hand, people choose leaders who have the enthusiasm for the lead; on the other, many of the most successful in life have the happy knack of appearing to have office thrust upon them.

Suppose that you interview someone for a job. Of course you will look for the specific qualities required for that particular post. But overall, and given a choice, you will pick the person who is really keen on the work, who is ambitious to succeed.

Electorates are rightly suspicious of those who have to be drafted. Voters with a cause – whether it be organisational, communal or financial – prefer the enthusiast, the campaigner, the fighter.

When I was after a certain elected post, I asked a shrewd American politician: 'How would you advise me to conduct myself?' He said: 'You want people to say: "It would be an honour to have him." If you are sufficiently distinguished in other spheres, they will want you out front in your own.

'So how do you achieve that apparent distinction? Choose to go out front on important issues and leave the trivia on one side; and when you appear in public and especially in photographs, do so with others who are more distinguished than yourself!'

Cynical, perhaps. But nevertheless correct. People like to share in honouring those whom others have found worthy of respect. Conversely, they are less likely to elect the unknown and certain to reject the apparently disreputable.

That said, there is no substitute for the personal approach, the request for support, the business equivalent of the election canvass. General and local elections are won and lost on the doorstep. 'All right,' says the voter, 'I'll support you. The other fellows haven't even bothered to come and see me.'

Of course, if issues are involved, it scarcely helps at election time to identify with the unpopular. Trimming is a political art, rightly regarded with disdain, but invariably practiced. There is no good reason why you should not emphasise the positive and eliminate the negative, and don't play with Mr In-between more than absolutely necessary. '

To be 'economical with the truth' is unwise, especially if you are forced into admitting your misdeeds. But equally, it is scarcely sensible to emphasise the gulf that may divide you from your voter. Anyway, the chair is placed into position as an acceptable bridge.

Finally, let us consider cases in which no vote is necessary. For instance – ten of you are sitting round a table for a general discussion. The group is too large for informality but too small to formalise. Volunteer the services of the most appropriate person – perhaps yourself.

'Go on Mary – take the chair. We need someone to create some sense in this meeting.' Or: 'We can't let this discussion ramble on. Shall I take the chair?'

There is no need for a formal vote – the position of chair is temporary and probably no one will object.

Do not feel that every decision must be made into a political contest – but be prepared to win if it comes to that. In meetings, as with elections, plan and prepare your case and your allies. Know what you want and plot how to get it. Do not be proud to ask for the votes you need. There is no joy in losing.

32 Resignations

Never resign!

To keep your legal rights when you lose your job, you do not resign. Otherwise (with rare exceptions) you are not 'dismissed' – 'wrongfully' or 'unfairly' or as 'redundant'.

To resign from the chair is (again, usually) an admission of defeat. Resigners lose.

In 1948, Manny (later Lord) Shinwell was Minister of War. Montgomery was refusing to pull British troops out of Palestine. Manny (I was told) threatened that unless they moved out in May, he would resign from the Cabinet and give his reasons.

Some years later, I asked Manny if this was true. 'It's absolute nonsense,' he said. 'I've never resigned from anything. If you do that, you lose. As a matter of fact, I've never threatened to resign, either. That is offering to lose. Your enemies will accept your offer and you are out.'

Resigners are losers. They may get momentary sympathy, but rarely any reward.

There are, of course, exceptions. Anthony Eden resigned on principle and came back to become Prime

Minister. But most politicians who voluntarily abdicate disappear into obscurity.

As with politics, local and organisational, national and international, so with business, the professions and any other organisation which you may chair. If you do not like the heat, by all means evacuate the seat; but recognise that you will no longer exercise that control which presumably you wanted, to achieve the organisation's purposes, or your own.

There are, of course, occasions when you should move temporarily out of the chair. Conflicts of interest are the commonest.

Perhaps you are involved in more than one organisation and their interests do not coincide. Then ask the vice-chairman to preside while the discussion proceeds.

Or if there are re-elections for your office, even if you know that you will be unopposed, arrange in advance for your deputy to take the chair during the discussion.

If you do decide to move out permanently, whether or not you intend to return, then plan your exit with care. Your method will depend on your intention.

It may be that you resign so as to draw positive attention to negative behaviour on the part of the organisation or a majority of its rulers. Then you may need the media to highlight your departure and to make the most of it. Your final act using the power of the chair will be to attract attention to your departure.

Conversely, you may want to leave in a way that will do the least harm to your name. Then you should seek ways to minimise the noise, to distract attention, to suggest that you are leaving by sensible consent and agreement and on good terms, individual and (if appropriate) financial.

So departures, like entries, need careful planning. There are always implications, organisational and sometimes financial. The art is to depart on the most acceptable basis.

Finally: make up your mind and do not keep changing it. If you have decided to resign, get on with it. If you are persuaded to change your mind, then give in – once.

But do not emulate the Italian Cabinet Minister who is said to have been given a chair with castors, so that he could more easily wheel himself in and out of the Cabinet room, each time he resigned!

Someone once said of David Lloyd George that he was likely to resign at any minute. 'Nonsense,' replied a more knowledgeable politician. 'He has two messengers at Number Ten. One is disabled, and he carries the letters of resignation towards Buckingham Palace; the other is a champion runner and he does the retrievals!'

Resignation, like litigation, should be a last resort for all who lead, not least from the chair.

33 Trespassers

From the chair, you regulate the meeting. Subject to a vote of no confidence, you are in charge. You dispense democracy, which means keeping order.

Plato described democracy as 'a charming form of government, full of variety and disorder, and dispensing a sort of equality unto equals and unequals alike'. That is the job of the chair. You dispense equality to those who do and who do not deserve it. They will produce a variety of responses and disorder is one of them. That you must control.

It has been suggested that if you want to understand democracy, you should spend less time in the library with Plato, and more time on the buses with people. The chairperson must understand how to control people. Which means the lawyers' fabled but non-existent 'man on the Clapham omnibus' – the ordinary, reasonable, average person. It also means disrupters.

People are likely to accept your control, if you exercise it; if you know what you want from them and from the meeting; if you listen to their views, dispense fairness and try to reflect the consensus of the meeting. But what of those who will not accept your rule or your ruling – who refuse to acknowledge even the basic procedures of the meeting? In this case you will normally have to rely on the laws of trespass.

Anyone who enters the property of another without consent or remains there after consent has been withdrawn becomes a 'trespasser'. It follows that you, as the presiding figure, may decide who is and who is not a trespasser.

Trespass is not a criminal offence; with rare exceptions, such as trespassing on a railway or military property, trespassers cannot be prosecuted. It is, though, a civil offence, which can lead to an action for an injunction or damages in a civil court.

If someone trespasses on property you occupy, you may sue in a civil court. Your two normal remedies are:

- an injunction, that is, an order of the court, restraining the trespasser from repeating his wrongful behaviour; and/or
- damages, that is, monetary compensation for the wrong done to you in your occupation of your land.

To ensure the smooth running of a meeting, when you don't have time to go to court, you have another remedy which is more immediate. You may use 'reasonable force' to evict a trespasser. How much force is 'reasonable' will depend on all the circumstances of the case. Ask the following questions:

- Have you tried to get the person to leave, without use of force?
- Was any force really required in order to 'abate the trespass'?
- How much physical force do you really need in order to get the trespasser to budge?
- Was any, and if so how much, force applied to you by the trespasser?

So what should you do if you are in charge of a meeting and a troublemaker refuses to leave? First, repeat your request to leave, firmly but politely. Then if that fails, make up your mind whether to leave the irritant in place or to ask a steward, or other strong citizen, to enforce your rule of law. If yours was a big meeting at which you might reasonably have expected disorder, then you should have planned for this eventuality in advance. Your stewards should be trained and skilled in the frog-march. As an alternative, or if an unacceptable level of struggle is offered to your bouncers (for that is their role, however unwanted) call the police.

It is not normally the job of the police to keep order at a private meeting, any more than it is in a private household. But they will intervene if there is violence in the home, and they should be prepared to help you if there is an actual or threatened breach of the peace at your meeting.

Force or the police, though, are (happily) rare and last resorts. The threat of eviction or (if necessary) to call the police is usually enough to deter even the most persistent disrupter.

34 Order! Order!

No meeting can succeed without order; and it is for the chair to maintain that order. The balance between freedom of speech and the maintenance of discipline is often precarious. In the words of Will Durant: 'When liberty destroys order, the hunger for order will destroy liberty'. The larger the meeting, the more unruly people you will attract. Your skills as chair will be tested – and if you lose command, the gathering will fall into the hands of the troublemakers. Allow your meeting to be destroyed by those who abuse their freedom to attend and to speak and you put democratic conduct of your meeting itself at risk.

As a start, the chair must convince the meeting that order is necessary for good reasons. Otherwise, the destructive will succeed.

George Bernard Shaw best summed up the legitimate view of the radical iconoclast: 'For the sake of society itself, it must be broken up.'

'Our laws make law impossible,' he said. 'Our liberties destroy all freedom; our properties organise robbery; our morality is an impudent hypocrisy; our wisdom is administered by inexperienced or mal-experienced dupes; our power is wielded by cowards and weaklings; and our honour is false in all its points. I am an enemy of the existing order for good reasons!'

You should do your best in the chair to ensure that those present do not feel enmity against the existing order; that if they wish to destroy it, they do so in accordance with its own rules; and that if they do not obey the rules, they are declared to be out of order.

The basic techniques depend upon the chairs' control of the meeting (see Chapter 5). But what can the law do to control those who seek to break up your meeting?

Let's start with order at a public meeting. Section 5 of the Public Order Act 1936 applies: 'Any person who in a public place or in any public meeting uses threatening or abusive or insulting words or behaviour in an attempt to provoke a breach of the peace or whereby a breach of the peace is likely to be occasioned shall be guilty of an offence.' If found guilty, the person may be sentenced to a fine of £50 or three months' imprisonment or both. A police officer may arrest any person 'reasonably suspected' to be committing an offence under Section 5, without warrant.

The same Section (as amended by the Public Order Act 1963, and by the Race Relations Act 1965) provides that anyone who uses 'threatening, abusive or insulting words or behaviour' in a public place or in any public meeting, or who displays any sign, writing or visible representation 'which is threatening, insulting or abusive, with intent to provoke a breach of the peace or whereby a breach of the peace is likely to be occasioned' is guilty of the same offence and liable to the same penalties.

Under the Public Meeting Act 1908, it is an offence to act in a disorderly manner at any public meeting, for the purpose 'of preventing the transaction of the business for which the meeting was called'.

The chair of a public meeting may call in the police and if a police officer 'reasonably suspects any person of attempting to break up the public meeting', the officer may order the interrupter to give his name and address. Failure or refusal to do so at once or the giving of a false

name or address is an offence. The policeman may arrest
a person who refuses to give particulars or whom he
reasonably suspects of providing false ones. No warrant
is needed.

So if you cannot yourself keep order and the meeting
is a public one, you may call in the police to assist you.
It is in the interests of the public that members of the
public shall be entitled to meet for lawful purposes. The
power of the chair is strengthened by the authority of
the law.

As a matter of tactics, of course, you should call in the
police only as a last resort. You will draw attention to
your own inability to control your own meeting; and the
disrupters will almost certainly attract exactly the media
attention which they wanted and you would rather have
avoided.

You must judge the alternatives, with care. There is
an old proverb: 'Of two evils, choose neither.' Unfortunately for the chair, when the choice lies between the
evil of the destruction of the meeting and the misery of
calling in the police, there is no choice other than to
choose.

What, then, are 'threatening, abusive or insulting
words or behaviour'? The phrase does not cover the out-
spoken dissenter, using blunt language but who does not
'threaten, abuse or insult'. On the other hand, while the
disrupter will be guilty of an offence if he deliberately
or intentionally disrupts your meeting, if the likely
result of his words or behaviour is to do so, that will
suffice.

These rules only apply to public (as opposed to private)
meetings. What is a 'public meeting'? It includes 'any
meeting in a public place and any meeting which the
public or any sector thereof are permitted to attend,
whether on payment or otherwise.' A 'public place' is:
'Any highway, public park or garden, any sea beach, and
any public bridge, road, footway, lane, court, square,
passage or alley, whether a thoroughfare or not; and
includes any open space to which, for the time being, the

public have or are permitted to have access, whether on payment or otherwise.'

In a nutshell, then, a public meeting is one to which the public are admitted or which is in a public place. It is therefore in the public interest that free speech should not deteriorate into disruption; and the rule of the criminal law, which is designed to set up minimum standards to protect the public, may be brought into force to supplement the rule of the chair.

PART FIVE

SPECIAL OCCASIONS

35 Chairing conferences

If you are taking the chair at a conference, where decisions will be taken on an array of different and specialised issues, then it makes sense to set up committees. The workload will be overwhelming. If you are to preside over the centre, delegate as much work as you can to the periphery.

If you are organising a large-scale conference (hereinafter, for convenience, referred to as 'a convention'), you will have to prepare for it. That job should be handed over to a *programme committee*. Its chair should be experienced and hardworking, acceptable and wise. Its members should be knowledgeable and flexible, reflecting the full range of those attending the convention.

A convention seeks a consensus. The programme committee is its microcosm. Include the young and the old, the left and the right, the traditional and the radical, in whatever sphere you cover. Propose them to your executive or other governing body. Better still, plant the proposals among those attending or get a respected but absent citizen to write a letter saying: 'I am sorry that I cannot be with you because of ... but I would respectfully suggest the setting up of a programme committee,

which might well include such redoubtable colleagues
as . . .'.

Flatter the 'colleagues' and they are unlikely to turn
down the invitation. Call them together not too often,
but always with a plan or a paper to discuss, paragraph
by paragraph, point by point.

It is the programme committee that should plot the
course of the convention, day by day, hour by hour. How
many speakers do you need and on what subjects? Who
is bright in both reputation and speech? Who will draw
the audience and prod their minds? Mix old stars with
young talent. Your programme should have as much
variety as commercial vaudeville. If you wish your delegates to be pleased, then instruct your programme committee to choose speakers who will not bore.

Well directed, the programme committee will ensure
that there are enough guests to provide novelty, but
sufficient time for the delegates to hear their favourite
sound, that of their own voices. They may have travelled
far for that joy. They may dine for ever off the tale of
how they held the floor at your convention. Then ensure
that your programme committee gives them their
minutes – but not other people's hours.

The programme committee should also decide on the
breakdown of meetings – into committees, sub-committees or (to use the current terms) 'workshops' or 'syndi-
cates'. The more numerous the groups, the greater the
number of speakers; the greater the number of speakers,
the greater the satisfaction.

Once the sessions are worked out, the programme committee will propose on whom the spotlight shall fall. In
particular: who will chair and who act as rapporteur,
bringing back the message of the minor group to the
mass of the plenary?

If lined up with skill and judgement, the speakers will
fill the bill, but not too much. The greatest problem is
inviting so many guests that they have no time to confer.
Remember that if you run out of guests, if your convention has any substance, you can usually find someone
substantial to fill the gap with distinction.

Next, select your *steering committee*. If you wish, your pre-convention programme committee can have new life as the steering committee, which will guide the gathering through its daily problems, arguments, disputes and procedural aggravations.

People who are good at planning in private and in peace may be poor in power or under pressure or in public. Or you may simply want to give extra glories to important people who need to be on committees to satisfy either their own vanity or pride or that of those whom they represent and who will be upset if their name does not appear on the printed programme. So you may prefer to have different faces on your steering committee.

Then you may need a *nominations committee*. This small but eminent body of leaders, selected from the top drawer, will decide whom to nominate for the various offices. In a controlled democracy, their nominees will probably get the jobs. In others, they will decide on and prepare the list of candidates. Or if nominations are received in advance, they will sort them out, and, together with the steering committee, set up the appropriate election procedures.

Finally, your convention may make resolutions. It may wish to summarise its view on key issues, either for its own benefit or (more likely) to put out to the press or public. In that case, create a *resolutions committee*. Its members should include people who are politically intelligent and experienced and linguistically articulate. A lawyer or two will do you no harm; plus a senior official of the organisation; and one or two people from your executive body. While all three other committees *should* be kept small, the larger the resolutions committee *must* be, the greater the task and the more likely the bungle.

When the resolutions committee has either decided or been instructed as to the nature of the resolutions required, it should delegate one or two of its members to put together the first draft. This is then brought to the committee, which knocks it into shape fit to go before the convention.

By creating and using these four committees, you

ensure adequate preparation by skilled people; proper
discussion in advance and at the time; a greater prospect
of success for the work of the convention; and a greater
spread of the blame in case of catastrophe. The larger the
convention, the more sensible the custom of organising it
through the committee system.

36 Administering conferences

The small, seemingly unimportant tasks in chairing a conference all add up to a massive responsibility – if any one thing goes wrong, you will be blamed. Plan carefully – and recruit others to help. But pay close attention to all the details yourself.

Whatever the nature or type of your conference, you must first decide: who should be in overall charge, holding the reins and making necessary decisions; and to whom the organiser will be responsible; how much independence he or she will be given; what reporting arrangements will be needed; and how the best communication will be achieved with the least misunderstanding.

Check the venue very carefully:

- Location: accessibility and convenience for the maximum number of attenders – including availability of road, rail or air services. You might want to meet at the company headquarters, at the most central location, or else in some unusual place to provide a change of scene and to honour some far-flung part of your organisation.
- Facilities: meals and refreshments, car parking,

clean and adequate toilets, plus swimming, golf, or
other recreation? Ensure that all your guests –
including the disabled – can participate fully.

- Equipment: chairs, tables, projectors, screens, amplification. Also, name tags, security passes, etc.
- Rooms for meeting and (if required) for sleeping:
  leave enough room to be flexible – if more people
  show up expectedly, or if you need space for extra
  sub-committees.
- Cost: as compared to other venues, including nature
  and extent of cancellation fees, extras, etc.
- Staff: adequacy, courtesy, efficiency and kindness of
  your helpers, including security officers, door attend-
  ants, and equipment technicians. If the conference is
  held in conjunction with an exhibition, then you need
  an expert – your own or hired – to plan, prepare, set
  up, supervise and dismantle the exhibits, collect,
  brief and otherwise prepare the exhibitors, and co-
  ordinate the entire operation.

Next comes the preparation of the programme and
speakers:

- What do you wish to achieve and how can it best be
  done, with maximum cost effect and minimum time
  and trouble?
- Which and how many speakers or presenters will be
  needed, and what will they charge?
- What documentation should be provided – and when
  – for example, for delegates to study beforehand (but
  who will do so, and who will forget to bring it with
  them?) and/or at the time and/or by way of follow-up
  – and who will draft and prepare it?
- Should delegates have a conference pack, with sched-
  ules, agendas, assessment sheets? What advertising
  or goods should delegates receive?

If you are marketing a conference for which those attending are expected to pay – whether on a break-even or
profit basis, then:

- What should you charge? What will people be prepared to pay and with what expectations?
- How do you gather in your delegates? What marketing material will you need, what will it cost, and who will prepare and print it and how will you put it before the eyes of your most likely punters, at minimum cost and with maximum effect?

When the event finally arrives, you will have to make many adjustments as it is in progress. Some important questions to bear in mind are the following:

- Are the guests being greeted on arrival? Do they have documentation, badges, refreshments, etc.? Are the VIPs receiving enough special attention?
- Is the seating satisfactory, or does it need shifting, perhaps during a coffee break? Can everyone see without discomfort? Are smokers separated from non-smokers, and with adequate ashtrays?
- How are the ventilation, amplification, heating, lighting?

Ensure you have enough staff on hand to help things run smoothly.

When the conference is over, that leaves the follow-up:

- Have the desired results been obtained, and how do you know? Who collects the assessment sheets and makes the appropriate appraisal?
- Will you need a follow-up conference – of organisers, participants or any (and if so, which) others – and when and who will prepare, address and brief it?
- Taking all the successes and failures, triumphs and errors into account, will you want a repeat, and, if so, on what basis, where, when and how? Especially, how will you avoid making the same mistakes again?

So before you physically take the chair, you must plan for the convention's success. The less you leave to chance, the greater your prospects of emerging with credit.

37 Chairing the company

Anyone may chair a company meeting, provided that he or she is elected to preside by the members (which means the shareholders) of the company. The Companies Act 1948, Section 134 says: 'Any member elected by the members present at a meeting may be Chairman thereof'. Which is all you will find about a company Chairman in the great mass of legislation about companies.

Instead, the company's duties are generally set out in its Articles of Association. Most companies adopt Table A of the Companies Act, which provides a standard form of rules for internal regulation.

Article 55 of Table A reads: 'The Chairman, if any, of the Board of Directors shall preside as Chairman at every general meeting of the company; or if there is no such Chairman or if he shall not be present within 15 minutes after the time appointed for the holding of the meeting or is unwilling to act, the directors present shall elect one of their number to be Chairman of the meeting.

'If at any meeting no director is willing to act as Chairman or if no director is present within 15 minutes after the time appointed for holding the meeting, members present shall choose one of their own number to be Chairman of the meeting.'

In most companies the chair of the company presides over annual, extraordinary and all other general meetings. It is the directors who decide on the chair, electing one of themselves to the job. Only in two cases will the shareholders be entitled to choose one of themselves to preside: if no director is present by a quarter of an hour after the time fixed for the start of the meeting; or if no director is prepared to act. The first circumstance could occur for any one of a variety of unusual reasons, from delay to disaster. The second is generally the result of dispute or other misery.

What, then, of meetings of the board itself? Once again, the chair of the company probably presides. If he is not present, then the directors will elect a chair from among themselves.

Table A (and most companies' Articles) provide that any question arising 'shall be decided by a majority of votes'. In case of a tie, the chair 'shall have the second or casting vote'. But a casting vote is only available if the Articles so provide. And it must not be used unless there is 'an equality of votes' and not (for instance) so as to achieve a desired deadlock.

In practice, votes at Board meetings are extremely rare. I can recall countless occasions when the chair has asked each person for a view, but I have never been present on any occasion when a vote has been taken at a board meeting. Only when a consensus is impossible and (for instance) the question of who chairs is an issue – or, on occasion, when the chair needs the clear, minuted and incontrovertible backing of the Board – is a vote at all likely.

With or without a vote, the chair must ensure that the meeting carries out its business without impropriety and in particular that 'the sense of the meeting is properly ascertained'. The opinions of those present must be sifted so that those who have met together (literally) have their say, and are heard. On the other hand, even a fair hearing has its limits. A minority should not (as de Tocqueville put it) 'tyrannise over the majority' by disrupting the meeting, filibustering or otherwise preventing those present from coming to a decision.

It is for the chair to ensure that motions or resolutions are put and discussed. The same applies to amendments. He or she must follow the rules – accepting resolutions and amendments which are presented in the proper way (see Chapter 29).

The chair may order a poll, in which votes are specifically recorded and counted. Once again, all depends on the Articles. If no poll is demanded or called, then the chair's decision as to the outcome of a vote on an extraordinary* or a special* resolution is conclusive. As to ordinary resolutions, the same rule generally applies and is embedded in the company's Articles of Association.

It follows that if you are in the chair at a company meeting of any sort and you preside over a vote, you must ensure that the proceedings are properly conducted; that all sides are heard; and if there is a deadlock, you will have a casting vote. You may decide 'incidental questions' which arise during the meeting.

You cannot normally adjourn a company meeting without consent, unless you need to do so to cope with disorder. If you try to adjourn without consent, then the meeting may elect someone else into your place and the business can proceed. Nor are you required to adjourn a meeting.

According to Article 57 of Table A: 'The Chairman may, with the consent of any meeting in which a quorum is present (and shall if so directed by the meeting), adjourn the meeting from time to time and from place to place. But no business shall be transacted at any adjourned meeting other than business left over from the meeting from which the adjournment took place.

'When a meeting is adjourned for 30 days or more, notice of the adjourned meeting shall be given as in the

---

* An 'ordinary' resolution normally requires 14 days' notice and may be passed by a simple majority. An 'extraordinary' resolution usually requires a larger majority – probably three-quarters – and 14 days' notice. A 'special' resolution needs 21 days' notice.

case of an original meeting. Save as aforesaid, it shall not be necessary to give any notice of an adjournment or of the business to be transacted at an adjourned meeting.'

The most quoted judicial dictum as to the proper conduct of a meeting is Lord Russell's statement, in 1937:

'There are many matters relating to the conduct of a meeting which lie entirely in the hands of those people who are present and who constitute the meeting. It rests with that meeting to decide whether Minutes or Notices, Accounts or Resolutions or such like shall be read to the meeting or taken as read; when discussions shall be terminated; and a vote taken; whether representatives of the press, or any other persons not qualified to be summoned to the meeting shall be permitted to be present or if present shall be permitted to remain; and whether the meeting shall be adjourned. . . . In all these matters, and they are only examples, the meeting decides; and if necessary, a vote must be taken to ascertain the wishes of the majority. If no objection is taken by any constituent of the meeting, the meeting must be taken to be assenting to the course adopted.'

In each case, it is for the chair to ensure that the meeting considers any problem in a proper way and comes to its decisions with due deliberation.

Now, resolutions. Normally, if there is a vote, then these are decided by a show of hands. A poll is a formal vote. Votes are generally inscribed 'for' or 'against' on papers duly signed by the individuals in person, or by proxy.

At a general meeting, a poll may be demanded either by the chair or by three or more members present, in person or by proxy, who represent not less than 10 per cent of the total voting rights, all the members having the right to vote at the meeting. A member or members holding shares in the company which confer the right to vote at the meeting on which an aggregate sum has been paid, equal to not less than 10 per cent of the total sums paid on all the shares conferring that right, may also demand a poll. Such a demand 'may be withdrawn' (Articles 58 of Table A). Article 61 provides that a poll

demanded on the election of a chair or on a question of
adjournment and which is not withdrawn must be taken
forthwith. On any other question, the person chairing
the meeting will direct when the poll shall be taken 'in
any business other than that upon which a poll has been
demanded may be proceeded with pending the taking of
the poll'.

Table A specifically gives the chair the right to order
the immediate removal of any person who seeks to dis-
rupt the meeting. Or he may adjourn the meeting, so
that 'the disorderly element' may be removed.

Those are the only references to the chair's duties
contained in Table A and thence in the Articles of Association of most companies. For further rules in your company, check its specific Articles. And if in doubt, consult
your company secretary or (if necessary) your lawyer.

Lord Milverton once said: 'The ideal committee is one
with me as Chairman and two other members in bed with
'flu.' Unfortunately, a chair can only operate a company
meeting if a quorum is present. And while in your
capacity as chair it is your job to ensure one person or
one share one vote, you cannot in law meet with yourself.

The story is told of a Soviet Jew, who had applied for
an exit visa. He was set upon by a gang of KGB men.
They threw him to the ground and twisted his arm
behind his back. Their leader shouted at him:

'What is the best country to live in?'

'The Soviet Union,' he replied.

'What country gives its citizens everything they need?'

'The Soviet Union, of course.'

'Where are all people happy and content?'

'The Soviet Union.'

'Which is the best country in the world?'

'The Soviet Union.'

'If those are your opinions, then why have you applied
to leave the Soviet Union?'

'Because I do not agree with my own opinions!'

If you are in the chair and on your own and do not
agree with yourself, then unanimity is impossible to

achieve. You should listen to others before making up your own mind.

In any case, when you are forced, knowingly, into a corner and you make a statement with which you personally disagree, leave yourself an escape route. Experienced politicians build open-ended phrases into controversial statements, providing themselves with a chance to retract or amend their opinion if necessary. Do the same!

38 Winning a beauty contest

Whatever your occupation, your business, your profession, you must sell to live. That means presentation in competition with others. In the City, this has become known as the 'beauty contest'. It must be won.

Often, a team presents itself as a commodity to a prospective client. The person in the chair is the key to winning. In that role you provide the flair and energy to maintain interest in the presentation and keep it running smoothly. Here are the essential rules.

First task: like the captain of a relay team, decide who goes first, second and third. The rule with relays is usually that you put your top runner (your chair) last, to overtake or to outstay the opposition; in general, your top performer should wind up your team presentation, leaving the right impression in the judges' minds.

The second best runner usually goes first, in order to give the team a head start over the competition. You should certainly put one of your accomplished colleagues up first, so as to set the scene, create the right atmosphere, and establish the best relationship with the judges.

Your necessary but pedestrian colleague – the person whose evidence is vital (otherwise he or she would not

be included in the team), but whose style of presentation
is inadequate – that person is sunk into the middle.
Hopefully, the information will remain alive, while the
memory of its package dies away.

Naturally, you vary these rules according both to the
content of and to your own part in the proceedings. Perhaps you will chair and kick off; or maybe you will
introduce briefly and then wind up. You must assess in
advance:

- how many presenters are required;
- their relative skills and importance;
- their running order;
- your own role and activity.

As chair and team selector, you are in charge of preparation. You must ensure that no one arrives unprepared
and that the presentations dovetail, one into the other.
Any overlapping must be deliberate, and designed (as,
once again, with the relay runners) to ensure a swift and
smooth handover.

Before making any presentation or speech, you must
always consider:

- Who is in the audience?
- What do they wish to hear?
- What will especially interest them? What should be
  emphasised?

Before a team presentation, discuss these essentials with
your colleagues and prepare together. Divide up the
material and then decide how to present it.

In particular: what visual aids will you require? Check
off the following:

- Documents: what should be put into writing and
  given to your potential clients or customers or other
  judges, and when? Which documents (if any) should
  they have in advance, at the time or to take away at
  the end?
- Flip chart – with pens?
- Overhead projector and transparencies?

- Slides?
- Rarer possibilities, such as computerised aids or autocue?

Make your preparation well in advance. Instruct your own graphics department or the agency that prepares your visual aids to provide you with proofs. Make sure that they are as professional as your outfit. Stint neither on your visuals nor on your documents.

Next: Take charge of rehearsals. Put yourself in the centre and your colleagues on either side. Go through the main points of your presentation and how they are to be placed before your particular audience. Above all – and most neglected by most beauty contestants – think of all the nastiest questions you may be asked; who will answer them; and how.

Rehearsing the horrors is an essential for all those who are likely to be interrogated in public. Prime ministers invariably spend hours with their colleagues and staff before their twice-weekly Question Time ordeal, planning how to deal with difficult bowling, how to avoid the googlies. Ambassadors, politicians, lawyers – all recognise that the dangers lie in the unexpected; and all try to ensure that all foreseeable expectations are guarded against, the best replies prepared in advance, the most impromptu responses plotted beforehand.

The greatest delight of a mischievous listener or judge is to prod differing and conflicting answers from a team of presenters. The chair must prevent this from happening. Consider, for instance, the following exchange, condensed, slightly exaggerated, but, otherwise typical, a group of professionals, (let's say engineers) pitching for a new account, and their potential client:

Client: 'How much will you charge for this job?'

Engineer A: 'It all depends how long it will take and who does it.'

Client: 'Yes, but we must have a very clear idea in advance or we can't plan our own costing.'

Engineer A: 'We'll provide an estimate.'

Client: 'How firm will the estimate be?'

Engineer A: 'Well, we can put an upper limit on it.'

Client: 'Please do so, then.'

Engineer B: 'We can't really put a firm upper limit until we know what will be involved. Your own requirements are likely to change as you go along.'

Client: 'But your colleague said you could put a firm upper limit.'

Engineer A: 'We can, but with reservations.'

Client: 'Oh, you have reservations now?'

Engineer B: 'Yes, but we can explain them.'

Client: 'Then how do you reach the figure to which you either can or cannot put a firm upper limit?'

Engineer A: 'It's based on the time taken by the people concerned.'

Client: 'So you cost out your time? On what basis?'

Engineer A: 'We don't normally reveal our precise method of costing.'

Client: 'Really? Do you expect us to take a pig in a poke?'

Engineer B: 'Well, we could tell you.'

Engineer A: 'But what you're really interested in is getting the job done at a reasonable cost and in the best possible way.'

Client: 'So you either are or are not going to tell us how you cost out your price or fees.'

Mistakes like this are as unfortunate as they are common. These can be avoided by careful preparation and, above all, by the chair taking charge. Do all in your power to ensure that such vital but often ignored questions about price or cost are anticipated and that the answers are prepared. Decide who will answer and how. Intervene and take over, with full authority, if there is the least hint that your colleagues do not know who will answer.

You are in charge. Presumably, you have been chosen because the ultimate responsibility for the job will be yours. You have to give your potential clients or customers the confident assurance of your competence and authority, or the contract will go to other contestants.

If a football team fails, the blame may fall on the

players. But the odds are that the captain, the coach or the manager will shoulder the responsibility. In a beauty contest situation, the role of all three is packed into the person in the chair. If you are in that seat, be aware of the problems and the responsibilities, and beware of the heat. It will be on you.

39 Meals and social functions

The Israeli statesman Shimon Peres gave up smoking. His staff told me that for the following two months, he was so irritable that they begged him to return to the weed, for the sake of the nation.

Not knowing of this new abstinence, I chaired a meeting for Peres in London. As a token of appreciation, I presented him with a parliamentary smoking set, complete with cigarette container and ashtrays.

If you chair you must prepare for the peculiarities of your guests. Do so carefully and kindly, without bringing undue attention to the problem.

Former American Secretary of State, Dean Acheson, once held a luncheon in the State Department. He had invited a group of youngsters, including the son of a friend of ours. The lad had a disabled right arm.

'How did it go?' my friend asked the boy, on his return home.

'Marvellous,' he replied. 'A miracle happened during the meal. They served steak. I was wondering how I was going to cut mine when Mr Acheson asked me to do him a favour. He said: "Johnny, your steak is done just as I like it. I wonder whether you would mind swopping with mine?" And you know what, Dad – his was already cut up!'

Concern for your guests, understanding for their peculiarities, their disabilities, their problems and their wishes, their dislikes – these lay the foundations for a successful beginning.

Consider: how many people will you ask? What do you wish to achieve and who should be there? What atmosphere do you seek and how can you best ensure it? What is the best venue? Will you sit around one table or many? Who will sit where and by whom?

Most people are extremely touchy about their position at a table. To avoid unnecessary trouble, diplomacy provides protocol. Basically, you should seat your guest of honour on your right; then the most important visitor on your left; your number two sits opposite you, with the next two guests in order of importance either side of him or her; then separate out the remainder, in order of importance and seniority and with your colleagues between them, leaving the least senior at the far ends.

Compatibility is more important at meals than at any other time – once seated there is no escape for your victims. Be careful.

When chairing an important dinner or other mealtime meeting, I arrange for a trusted colleague to do the first draft of the seating plan, but I always check it. Protocol and pride come first; pleasure and companionship follow close behind. It never helps to seat a guest at the side of his mortal enemy. Poison comes from people more than from food.

If the occasion is large, try to avoid top table. Instead, why not seat the guest speaker beside you, in a table at the centre, with distinguished colleagues at different ends of the table – or different tables, spread through the room?

Choose a room that is full. Speakers must be seen as well as heard; and to fill is to fulfil. Empty spaces have no place in mealtime meetings.

Check and recheck your seating plan and allow for last minute errors and changes. At many well-run governmental and official meals, each guest is provided with a copy of the seating plan and with a list of fellow guests, with short biographies or résumés.

Brief speakers. Tell them in advance to whom they will be talking: about what: for how long: and for what purpose.

Make sure that your speakers are heard and that microphones and (if appropriate) visual aids are available and properly and conveniently placed.

Consider documentation. Will guests need organisational information, briefing or promotional material?

Then plan the talk. American Supreme Court Justice Frankfurter was once found sitting in his car, outside the home where he was to dine. 'Why aren't you coming in, Justice?' his host enquired.

'Sorry to keep you,' he replied. 'I am just preparing my conversation.'

When you are in the chair, prepare yours. Will you talk business at the beginning or at the end? Will you introduce the guests or the organisation formally, after coffee, or between courses?

At a Belgian banquet, I found that I was to speak between the main course and the sweet. I misquoted the words of French King Louis XIV: *'Après moi le dessert!'*

The larger the occasion, the more careful the protocol. Will there be a loyal toast? It should precede both smoking and coffee. If the session is lengthy, then allow a pause for your guests to visit the spa or other watering place.

Above all, stick to time. From the chair, you decide whether or not your guests are late for their appointments – whether they are going to stay happily until the predetermined end, or drift apologetically away – and whether they will return for future meals, in the expectation of pleasure, or stay away in the fear of fatigue.

Far too many chairs take far too many mealtime occasions for granted. It is not enough to welcome, to compére and to bid farewell. It is for you to ensure that the occasion is fully and properly planned and prepared or to ensure that someone else does so. Samuel Pepys wrote in his diary: 'Strange to see how a good dinner feasting reconciles everybody.' It is your job to make sure the dinner is good.

Finally, try to match the menu to the preferences or cultural and religious requirements of (at least) your guests. When that is not possible and an inappropriate dish is served to a reluctant diner, have the food removed – without fuss or commotion. Your guest will appreciate your diplomacy.

40 Creditors' meetings

Neither a debtor nor a creditor be. But if you are either, you may have the misfortune to attend a creditors' meeting. Only if you are an accountant will you chair it.

Still, as an illustration of the variety of situations in which special rules of chairing need studying and following, let us consider the chairing of a creditors' meeting. I am indebted to Mr David Lovett, of Arthur Anderson & Co., a specialist in this macabre field, for his advice in preparing this chapter.

Most chairs are nominated, elected, accepted and retained by those over whom they preside. Not so the chair of a creditors' meeting, who is normally nominated to act as liquidator by the shareholders (or members) who are also the directors. However, the purpose of the meeting is to give the creditors an opportunity to question the directors about the stewardship of the company. The creditors then have the chance to nominate their own liquidator. So the chair has relied on the directors for instructions to date; and will rely on the creditors for his or her future appointment.

What, then, are the rules you should follow, as chair, in this especially exposed and perilous position?

- Be and appear to be *independent*.
- Brief the directors in advance, to give full *answers* to questions asked.
- If directors are evasive, then *assist the creditors*. For instance, remind the creditors of their previous words.
- Keep yourself and the meeting cool: *stop* any creditor or director who becomes *offensive*.
- Ensure that questions asked are *relevant* to the matters at issue.
- Know the *law* and *procedures*, especially during any voting.
- Above all, *be firm and fair*.

As you will see, most of the rules which apply to this specialised meeting are simply variants of the general, the normally necessary. But the more exposed or potentially controversial your position – the more vulnerable you may be through actual, apparent or possible conflicts of interest – the more carefully you must tread.

A well-known novelist was in deep debt. A creditor stopped him in the street. 'Where's my money?' he demanded.

'I'm sorry,' said the novelist, 'but I have no money. Please be patient.'

'That's exactly what you said to me a month ago.' said the creditor.

'Well I have kept my word!' proclaimed the novelist.

Those who demand the trust of creditors or debtors must likewise keep their word. To succeed in the chair of a creditors' or of any other meeting, trust matters.

41 Ceremonial and commercial

With a roll of drums and a fanfare of trumpets, the chair marches to the centre of the platform. Behind him, high on a screen in the darkened room, flash the name and the logo of the company. Speaking from invisible notes on his autocue, the executive tells his story, proclaims the company's successes, acclaims winners of awards, presents his greetings, his salutations, and his gifts to the worthy.

With every cost lavished, the chair has become part of a modern spectacular, of an audio-visual experience, professionally produced and royally rendered. If it is properly prepared and well delivered, the speech is the centre of the message. The rest is vivid illustrations. If it is delivered in an embarrassed monotone, its deficiencies are exaggerated by their unhappy contrast with the brilliant audio-visual effects. Conversely, many an excellent speech has been ruined by inadequate, unsuitable or inappropriate slides, by over-amplification or by obtrusive music, by visuals that are intended to aid but in fact hinder.

If you have to make an important presentation of this kind, it is not enough to hire in top experts. You must prepare yourself and them; check all their materials as well as your own; and try to achieve a balance.

As the speechmaker and most important presenter, you are both soloist and conductor. In your first role, you must both stand out and be outstanding – allow neither yourself to be cast into darkness nor your words into the background. In your second role, you must ensure that your Light and Sound show is co-ordinated, so that the ears and the eyes of your audience combine to transfer your message to their emotions and to their intellects.

You have renounced the simplicity of the simple speech for the complication of the staged production. You are in the world of show business and will need producers, directors, light and sound engineers, machinery and equipment to work in harmony.

Cost apart, this sort of modern speechmaking should either be well prepared and expertly performed, or avoided completely. Too many people who are thrust into speechmaking believe that by handing over the production to experts, they can hide in the shadows, read scripts prepared for them by others, and simply take the applause. Too often, the result is disastrous.

For example, a top City financial institution invited Members of Parliament from all parties to a presentation and dinner in a Westminster hotel. To their delight, over 100 accepted.

The opening cocktail reception went well. The victims were then duly herded into the dining room and seated at their tables, one executive at each. The presentation was dreadful. We endured a series of speeches, read by the chairman and two of his colleagues, to the background of lush, logoed slides.

Our hosts should have asked the four questions:

- Who are the audience?
- Why are they here and what do they want from us?
- What is our message – what do we want to put across to them?
- How do we drive home that message?

They had answered the third question. They wanted to

show us the size, strength and structure of their set-up, to convince us of its heritage of excellence. They had decided to spread their message orally, using their topmost senior people, and visually, by modern techniques. They had answered the first question – they knew who we were, and how to attract us. The second question, which is the most important, they had totally forgotten.

After all, why should such a large number of legislators wish to spend an evening with them? We would all enjoy a good meal and most would happily swallow a few drinks. But few of us were totally undernourished or dehydrated. What we wanted was to tune in on our hosts' view of the economy, their explanation for past events, their vision of the future. We wanted our questions answered, even if they went unasked. Instead, we were served up with a droning monotony of voice, to a background of well-produced irrelevancies. Not one of us cared about their pyramid of management strength, the growth in their turnover, the monumental architecture of their new premises.

So the opportunity and the money were wasted. Modern technology destroyed the communication, the presentation, the speeches.

By contrast, I enjoyed a brisk presentation by an hotel company. Drum rolls, fanfare, name and logo, flashes of hotels – all were there, along with a succulent buffet. Both speakers were spotlighted; they spoke well, voices and eyes raised. The Minister of Tourism spoke briefly and clearly. He presented flags to the hotel managers. The three *E*s flowed through the event – energy, excitement and enthusiasm. The combination of classic speechmaking and technological miracles can produce high impact. Misused, it can destroy. Our City hosts would have done much better to stand on the stage; to ask what questions we wanted answered; then to field them, with skill and authority. Instead, they ate the poisoned apple which killed off their occasion.

Learn, please, from their mistakes.

Checklist for the chair

Once you have read this book, use it for reference. The contents and the index are your guides. But here is a brief guide which covers the most important points. Neglect these at your own peril:

- The chair arbitrates the proceedings and must avoid becoming involved directly in the issues being discussed. Maintain your fairness and impartiality, and keep your cool at all times. Be patient and use plenty of humour.
- Show your confidence – real or not. Sit up straight, look at your audience, and keep authority. Concentrate and you will not lose the respect of your colleagues.
- Plan your speeches well in advance. Decide how to convey your message clearly and persuasively. Use brief notes, and allow for flexibility as you speak. Arrange your props and equipment beforehand. Talk clearly and loudly.
- Set out your goals in advance, and plan the agenda carefully so that you can move the meeting towards winning your goals without losing your apparent impartiality. Explain the agenda to the participants.

- Decide who should speak on each issue, and maintain a balance. Do not prevent a person from speaking, even if he attacks you personally.
- Know and enforce the proper rules for tabling resolutions, motions and amendments. Try to keep these procedures to a minimum – they take up valuable time.
- Ensure that the official minutes are accurate and fair. Appoint an ally to record them, for this purpose will wield considerable power over the results of the meeting. In any case, check their accuracy.
- When faced with hostility, listen patiently, apologise, and offer alternative solutions. Treat your enemies with courtesy and defeat them by careful planning, not by force. If they win, back down gracefully and you will not lose the confidence of your colleagues.
- Handle disruptors with strength. Do not lose control of the situation. An amateur heckler can be silenced with a short jibe. Serious and determined disruptors should face the rules of the meeting. If this method fails, evict them with force, or even call in the police. The law is on your side.
- Threaten to adjourn the meeting when your enemies are gaining the upper hand. If they continue, postpone the meeting until a time when you can bring in your supporters.
- Never resign. You will lose all control over the proceedings.

So, if genius is only 90 per cent inspiration, chairing is 90 per cent preparation. Use this list to check that yours is well done.

Chapter Summaries

1 Qualities of the chair

- The chair must be fair – for you must dispense justice and keep the trust of your colleagues and the audience.
- To control a meeting, the chair must have self-control. Do not openly take sides and never lose your temper.
- Think clearly and objectively. Keep your goals in mind, and do not get bogged down in red tape or petty disputes.
- Stay aware of the rules and procedures of your organisation. You will need to wield them swiftly and accurately.
- Maintain a sense of humour, for otherwise you will crack.

2 Where the buck stops

- The chair takes some of the credit and all of the blame, so be prepared to do a good job.

150

- Learn from past experience. Try to repeat your successes without repeating your errors.
- Compare your performances to those of other chairs. Strive to do better.
- Be confident – or at least pretend to be.
- Your good name, and that of your organisation, are the most important attributes to preserve. Keep this goal in mind.

3 Listening and judging

- Keep an open mind – and open ears. Listen to others, for they hold the key to your success. Ignore them and you will fail.
- Keep notes when other people speak. You will flatter them, and will not forget what they said.
- Use your common sense. Bring your personal experience and knowledge to the meeting.

4 Fairness

- When you make decisions, explain your reasoning. You must appear completely open.
- Ensure that all viewpoints are heard. Make sure that everyone has a chance to speak, and they will accept the final decision with good grace.
- Your audience must believe that justice has been done. Without this trust, you will have no authority.

5 Leadership and teamwork

- Adapt your leadership style to suit the occasion and the mood of your audience.
- Clearly lay out your goals – and keep them in mind.
- Decide whether to take a dominating role or simply to moderate.

- Make sure that the rest of your team is prepared and ready to work together effectively.
- Your colleagues must know the role of every other member of your team and keep their concentration even when not speaking – otherwise they will be caught up in contradictions and lies.
- Leave your audience with your goals in mind.

6 The autocrat

- Do not become a dictator – or even seem like one. You will quickly alienate your colleagues and your audience.
- If you must dominate from the chair, explain why. Never become overbearing.

7 When the chair speaks

- Prepare your speeches carefully and well in advance. Decide what you will say, what equipment you will need, etc.
- Ensure that you have prompted your allies in the audience, especially the person who will introduce you.

8 Structuring speeches

- Plan out your speeches in advance, keeping a basic outline on small notecards.
- Do not read from a text – you will need to judge your audience and be flexible as you speak.
- The start and the finish are the most important parts of any speech. Begin by setting a positive atmosphere and make sure that you end on a high point.

9   Wit and humour

- Spontaneous, witty humour quickly revitalises sleepy audiences. A clever phrase can disarm your opponents and gain more allies.
- Avoid offensive jokes if possible. If you must be crude or derogatory, make sure your audience understands your true intentions.
- Tease your audience, but do so carefully. Again, make sure you are not offending anybody, even unintentionally.
- If your humour is failing – if your audience is very serious – then switch it off as long as they stay interested.
- Poke fun at yourself. No one will be offended. You can downplay your faults and emphasise your best qualities without seeming pompous.

10   Body language

- The chair sets the tone of the meeting. Make your audience feel welcome by smiling as they come in – and nodding your head at important arrivals.
- Appear confident – sit upright or lean back casually but with authority. Do not slouch or hang your head over your notes without looking up.
- When opening a meeting, stand up or rap your gavel on the table. Take command, rather than waiting for silence.

11   The voice of authority

- The chair must be heard, clearly and with presence. Speak loudly, so the deaf man in the last row can hear you.
- If necessary, get a trusted colleague to signal from the rear if you are too quiet or too loud.

12   The pause

- Use pauses to focus attention on yourself. When you bring a meeting to order, let silence fall on the room briefly and you will have everybody anticipating your first words.
- Pause before crucial words or phrases to give them particular emphasis.
- After a long or dull speech, a brief pause will put energy into the room again. Give people time to stretch, yawn, and force blood back into their brains.
- Allow your audience breathing time as you speak. Talk normally, pause after major points, and people will absorb much more.
- If you lose concentration, or get asked a tough question, do not plunge ahead without thinking. A short pause to collect your thoughts will make you much more articulate – and you will seem more thoughtful and wise.

13   Fighting your nerves

- Never let your mind wander. If you lose concentration, the unexpected will find you totally unprepared.
- Concentration will keep you in control – and it will banish nerves. If you wallow in anxiety you will end up making mistakes. Think only about what is at hand.
- Try to appear confident – however nervous you are. Make eye contact with your audience, speak loudly, hold yourself up, and others will take notice. Once you get going, your nerves will stop shaking.

14   Props

- Keep with you the essential documents you will refer to during the meeting – the agenda, names of speakers, and notes you will need. Make sure they are all in order and accessible.

- Have an assistant ready to lend a hand.
- Use a lecturn for long talks, when the speaker is handling lots of papers, or when a microphone and light stand is necessary. However, do not create a barrier between the audience and you.
- Minimise distractions for the speaker. Test the lighting and amplification long before the meeting starts.
- Your notes should be clear and concise, detailing only the main points in an easily-legible format. Use small cards which can be rearranged or easily added to.
- Do not allow others to prepare your notes.
- Do not stare down at your notes – look out at your audience.

15 Introductions

- Introduce yourself even if only a few people do not know you. Give your position in the organisation and a few words on yourself, perhaps in jest.
- Keep notes on the person you are to introduce – write down even the person's name. Under pressure, you will forget it.
- Say a few flattering remarks about your guest speakers. Ask them what they would like said, and embellish it. And do some research into their accomplishments – they will appreciate it.
- Avoid clichés – a particular temptation when giving introductions (or any other stylised speech).

16 Structuring your meetings

- Base your meetings around a well-prepared agenda, but think about the unexpected directions the meeting could go, and plan for them.
- Explain the structure to all your colleagues, both

to ensure their full participation and to win their
confidence.

17 Compromise

- The goal of the chair is to reach a compromise – a
  final decision acceptable to all.
- You must use patience and barter to reach a solution,
  but in the chair you also have the power to move
  negotiations towards your viewpoint.
- Do not humiliate the loser. You may need his services
  later, so keep him happy – allow him some conces-
  sions – and he will support you.
- Similarly, do not refuse to back down on a minor
  point. Yield a small concession now, and you may
  win a larger one later.

18 Who speaks?

- As a subject approaches, consider who should discuss
  it. Alternate between supporters and opponents. Give
  your allies ample warning.
- Balance the speakers in favour and against. You
  must appear to be fair – even if you support one side.
- You might want to recognise only the speakers who
  support you, or who are weak opponents. Use selective blindness, but do not entirely exclude a person
  from the floor without good reason.
- According to the circumstances, allow your main
  opponent to speak as much as necessary. Arrange the
  counter-attack once he has exhausted his argument.
- Deciding who shall speak, the chair must remain
  courteous and caring. Do not provoke hostility.

19 Handling disruption

- There are many kinds of troublemakers, and each should be handled differently.
- The person who disrupts the session for fun should be handled with his own medicine. Keep cool, and send a few jibes back at him. If he persists, you will have the rest of the audience on your side and you can safely silence him.
- Keep your sense of humour, but always make it clear that you will assert your authority when necessary. Never lose control of your temper – for then the heckler will have won.
- Be firm when a heckler is disrupting someone else's speech. Do not humour him – silence him quickly, using the rules of the meeting.
- When a disrupter is bending the rules in his favour by calling for endless points of order or tabling countless amendments, be patient and get some trusted ally to suggest a close to the business. You can also refer the matter to a sub-committee.

20 Coping with anger

- When faced with hostility, do not argue back. Listen to and show your respect for other views.
- Apologise – regardless of who is to blame.
- Offer alternative solutions or consolations, and make sure that the disgruntled person receives the services that you have promised.
- Take special care of people who hold a grudge against you. Watch them closely, and do not give them further reasons to be angry.

21 Opponents and enemies

- In the chair, you must ensure that people respect you and your decisions. Do not make enemies.

- Treat your enemies with courtesy. Be patient and do not interrupt. Avoid being drawn into the conflict. At least, agree to disagree.
- Before the meeting, figure out who your enemies are likely to be – and how you will deal with them. Do not be caught off guard.
- Do not expel opponents from the meeting – they will move the conflict into a more public arena. Similarly, do not resign – you will lose all control over the proceedings.
- Lose gracefully. Do not stake your authority on winning a single issue. When you lose, simply move onto another issue without holding a grudge.

22   Plants – and their dangers

- To win from the chair, you will need allies among the participants. Plant them strategically, and coach them well in advance.
- Signal your allies when you want someone to propose closing a debate, calling for a vote, or adjourning the meeting. Be sure to maintain the impartiality of the chair.

23   Interruptions

- Interruptions revitalise dull meetings and can provide opportunities to state your case more clearly.
- When heckled, use the chance to refute the arguments of your detractors directly. A little humour will gain you the sympathy and support of the rest of the audience.
- Avoid becoming distracted or confused by outside interruptions. Patiently wait for the passing fire engine to go by – and then make a clever joke to bring attention back to ourself once you can be heard again.

24 Time management

- Everything takes longer than it should, so allow for over-running. When stretched, cut back on the formalities and allow time for the substantive discussions.
- Tell your speakers they have less time than you have actually allocated.
- When speaking yourself, watch your audience. If it is bored, finish speaking quickly – or improve the quality of what you are saying. From the chair, quietly encourage dull speakers to wind up. Arrange a signal to give when a speakers' time is up – and don't be afraid to use it.
- During long sessions, allow time for a coffee break or a walk around. Do not make your audience feel uncomfortable and trapped.

25 Precedents

- Follow in the path of tradition – it is the easiest route. But do not be afraid to explore in new directions when necessary.
- From the chair, most of your decisions will be based on precedents. Your job is to select the precedent that will achieve your goals.
- When faced with iconoclastic radicals, invoke precedents to defeat their changes.
- Defeat traditionalists by finding the tradition that suits your case. Prepare your arguments well in advance – the old guard have far better memories of what they did than you have.

26 The agenda

- The agenda is the route map of the meeting. As the chair, check it carefully before proceeding. Decide what you want to achieve – and what you want to exclude.

- Decide whether to put contentious matters at the beginning or the end. How long should they be discussed – should there be a full debate or should you cut it short? Should you leave the matter off the agenda entirely, hoping it will be forgotten?
- Consider the time available. Do not crowd too much into the meeting – or leave too much uncontrolled free time. Have room for flexibility.

27 Minutes

- Carefully check over the minutes of past meetings. They are the only permanent record of what occurred.
- The person who prepares the minutes has vast powers to alter the decisions that were taken. Do not have opponents take them.
- Different organisations have different ways of keeping minutes – from a short summary of votes, to a verbatim record of everything said.
- The minutes should be prepared immediately after the meeting, when memories are fresh and people have time to review them. Allow people to check the minutes before they are circulated, but do not automatically allow them to make changes.
- In disagreements, the chair must negotiate a settlement between people with differing recollections. The sooner the minutes are agreed to, the less chance of such conflicts.

28 Adjournments

- The chair's greatest power is the ability to adjourn. Use it as a threat, and as a practical weapon.
- To silence an opponent, suggest returning on another day to finish the discussion. Most people will quieten down and get it over with.

- If you are losing your case, adjourn to another time when you can rally your allies and overcome your challengers.

29 Resolutions, motions and amendments

- Some resolutions are only in order if they are on the agenda, so that the opponents will know to attend. In some cases, emergency resolutions may be acceptable. The chair – and the rules of the meeting – make the decision.
- Ensure that each motion has a proponent and a seconder. Call for a debate, alternating between speakers in favour and opposed. Include undecided speakers as well.
- When there are no more speakers, let the proponent have a final say. If there is a closure to debate, allow each side a final speech.
- When possible, ban resolutions and amendments. They take up valuable time and slow down more important proceedings. At least, limit the time you allocate to debates and try to put a stop to endless amendments.
- Resolutions can be used to speed up a meeting by forcing the participants to focus on a single written document.
- Each amendment must be debated in the same way as the original resolution.
- Amendments must be voted on before the resolution itself. The resolution then stands for a vote only after it has been amended.

30 Votes

- The chair might vote as any other participant, or might never vote, or might vote in case of a tie – according to the rules and traditions of the meeting.
- Most votes will be by show of hands. Only in rare

cases – when a vote is very close or when a record of
each person's vote is necessary – should a formal
ballot be used. Ballots are necessary in secret votes.
- Be prepared for a ballot, by having paper and ballot
boxes ready. Appoint tellers to count the results.
- The chair announces the results with or without the
exact number of votes.

31 Elections

- To win an elected office you must have the courage
to ask people to vote for you. Do not be too proud,
otherwise you will not win.
- Take the time to canvass. Personally speak to as
many voters as possible and explain why you are the
best candidate.
- Standing for office, appear enthusiastic and
ambitious. Associate yourself with powerful and
respected people. Highlight your strong points, and
do not pursue unpopular causes.

32 Resignations

- Do not resign. You lose all power over decision-
making and gain nothing beyond momentary sympathy. Resign only if you plan to leave the organisation entirely, and want to attract as much attention
as possible.
- Resign temporarily to avoid conflicts of interest, for
instance during the election of officers or when
making decisions on another organisation you are
involved with.

33 Trespassers

- In private meetings, the chair can legally exclude the
uninvited or the unwelcome. Have them thrown out

or call the police. You can secure an injunction and sue for damages.

- If you treat your enemies with care, you will not need to exercise this power. Try patience and courtesy first.

34 Order! Order!

- Public meetings are difficult to control. In theory, everyone is welcome to participate fully – and they often do. The chair must strike a balance between democracy and order.
- The chair has the authority to exclude from any public meeting people who are insulting or abusive, or who attempt to prevent the meeting from taking place.

35 Chairing conferences

- When many different and complicated issues are to be discussed with you in the chair, careful preparation is crucial. Delegate to committees the authority to plan the event.
- Create a programme committee to oversee the whole conference. It will decide the number of speakers, the number of delegates, and the composition of sub-committees. Appoint representatives from all factions of your group.
- The steering committee will guide the event as it occurs – running from crisis to crisis making sure it does not fall apart.
- A nominations committee should decide the candidates who will stand for each office.
- The resolutions committee will co-ordinate decision-making at the conference. Appoint politically sensitive people and lawyers, if possible.

36 Administering conferences

- The chair must carefully orchestrate the small
  details that lead to the success or failure of a conference. Decide who will be in charge of the
  administration.
- Before the conference, find the appropriate venue,
  with a good location, adequate facilities for all the
  delegates, and plenty of staff – all at a reasonable
  cost.
- Prepare advertising to attract potential delegates,
  and ensure that they have all the important information when they arrive.
- Hire enough assistants to troubleshoot during the
  conference, greeting delegates, moving chairs, photo-
  copying, and guarding the doors.
- Follow up the conference by surveying the delegates,
  asking whether your goals were met, and deciding
  how to avoid the same problems next time.

37 Chairing the company

- Anybody can be the chair of a company meeting,
  provided he or she is elected by the shareholders. The
  same person presides over meetings of the Board,
  although in his absence another member will be the
  chair.
- The chairman must ensure that the preceedings are
  fair and equitable to all parties.
- In most companies the chairman has a deciding vote
  in cases of a tie. Polls, recording the votes of each
  person present, may be called by the chairman or by
  a group of the members.
- The chairman can not normally adjourn a meeting
  unless it is necessary to maintain order. If a meeting
  is adjourned to another time or place, only business
  carried over from the original meeting may be discussed. If adjourned by over 30 days, written notice
  of the second meeting must be distributed.

- The chairman has the authority to remove any disruptive person from the meeting.

38 Winning a beauty contest

- In giving a presentation, the chair holds most responsibility for conveying a positive image. The chair leads the team.
- Decide the order in which your team will speak. Generally, end with the most effective speaker and begin with the next best. Take into consideration their special skills and especially the nature of the information they are to deliver.
- Gear your presentation to suit the audience. Think about what you want to tell them, and what they want to hear.
- Decide what kind of visual aids and documents you will need to use – and allow time to prepare them.
- Rehearse and plan speeches individually before giving the presentation. Make sure that speakers fully understand the positions of their colleagues so that they will not overlap or contradict each other. If there are problems, the chair must intervene to make matters clear.

39 Meals and social functions

- Prepare social occasions very carefully. Every guest will have particular likes and dislikes – your job is to make sure that each one is happy.
- Be extremely patient and understanding of everybody's foibles – and be flexible enough to adapt when problems occur.
- Special care is needed when seating people around a dinner table – once in place, your guests are trapped. Follow closely the rules of protocol in putting people in positions of honour, but do not neglect considerations of pleasure and companionship.

- Brief your speakers carefully so they are not caught unprepared. Set up all the equipment you might need – projectors or a microphone – well in advance so that you will not interrupt the meal to prepare for the speakers.

40   Creditors' meetings

- Creditors' meetings are just one example of how the rules of chairing are so important.
- The chair is put into place to give the creditors a chance to question the directors of a company in debt. Neither side wants to be there – so your skills as a patient arbitrator will be tested.
- Know the rules and procedures that govern the meeting. Remain independent. Ensure that questions are asked fairly, and the answers are honest and true. Calm down hostile participants by being firm and fair.

41   Ceremonial and commercial

- Whether presenting awards and salutations or proclaiming your company's successes against a spectacular audio-visual background, ensure that your speech is properly prepared and well delivered. The rest, then, is vivid illustration. If, however, you speak in an embarrassed monotone, the deficiencies of your speech are exaggerated by their unhappy contrast with the audio-visual effects.
- When making an important presentation of this kind, it is not enough to hire in the experts. You must prepare yourself and them; check all their materials as well as your own; and try to achieve a balance.
- Ask the four questions: Who are your audience? Why are they here and what do they want from you? What

is your message to them – how do you put it across?
How do you drive the message home?

Index

169